BINGO NIGHT

at the fire hall

Rediscovering Life
in an American Village

A HARVEST BOOK ● **HARCOURT BRACE & COMPANY**

barbara
holland

B
I
NIGHT
G
O *at the fire hall*

San Diego ● New York ● London

Requests for permission to make copies of any part of the work should
be mailed to:

Permissions Department, Harcourt Brace & Company,
6277 Sea Harbor Drive, Orlando, Florida 32887-6777.

Library of Congress Cataloging-in-Publication Data
Holland, Barbara.
    Bingo night at the fire hall: rediscovering life in an American
village/Barbara Holland. — 1st ed.
        p.   cm.
    ISBN 0-15-600665-0 (pbk.)
    ISBN 0-15-100268-1
    1. Loudoun County (Va.) — Social life and customs.   2. Blue
Ridge Mountains Region — Social life and customs.   3. Country
life — Virginia — Loudoun County.   4. Holland, Barbara.   I. Title.
F232.L8H65   1997
975.5'28 — dc21   96-53867

The author thanks *Mid-Atlantic Country, Country Journal*, and *AGE
Monthly* in whose publications some sections of this book originally
appeared in a different form.

Text set in Electra
Designed by Rich Hendel
Printed in the United States of America
First Harvest edition 1999
E   D   C   B   A

To the Last Villagers

contents

· · · · · · · · · · · · · · · ·

B
I
N IGHT
G
O *at the fire hall*

coming from away

....

Mondays and Fridays I go down into the valley to the offices of the county newspaper and write obituaries. Friends think this must be depressing, but it isn't. So many of my subjects die peacefully at home and full of years, to be borne by a full count of pallbearers to the churchyard beside the village church, that death here wears an almost grandfatherly face.

When relatives of the deceased call or stop by the paper to drop off a photograph or correct the spelling of a name, details slip out. One woman was killed in a fall when her horse shied; she was ninety-one. Another, aged ninety-four, died shortly after serving and eating Thanksgiving dinner, having assembled her many descendants for final instructions.

I study the photographs. Some of them are laminated driver's licenses; some family snapshots, peeled out of an album for the occasion, and the BarcaLounger, the television set, and somebody's shoulder will need to be cropped out. Women are often photographed in their kitchens, part of a refrigerator showing behind them. One elderly gentleman had a gray cat cuddled on his shoulder that couldn't be cut and ended up included. Often there's a Christmas tree in the background or a birthday cake in the foreground, and sometimes the whole family has pressed together to be photographed in front of the house; the deceased is second from the left.

"Survivors include," I write, and list them all, the nieces, the great-grandsons, the sisters-in-law. I list where they live. They live here. Some of them have clustered in a single town; others are sprinkled up and down the valley in village and town and hamlet, but nobody will need to drive more than twenty minutes to the funeral, and some will be able to walk to it.

Very occasionally a Florida address will turn up, representing older relations, driven south like robins from our bitter winters; in summer they've appeared in the paper's social columns, home visiting family around the valley, sleeping in a series of family guest rooms, staying in homes only five or six miles apart.

I have changed worlds, and nothing about this strange place seems stranger than this, in eastern America, at the end of the twentieth century, when the very word "local," as in "local strawberries" or "a local boy," is fading from the language.

I'm afraid it speaks badly for the professional attainments and ambitions here. No corporation has bothered to lure our people to Houston or Chicago; no one has found a challenging job in Silicon Valley, or even across the river in Washington. What work they do, they can do here at home.

Basically everyone who has made it past the age of eighty-

. . . . .

five was a farmer or a farmer's wife. Some of them are nudging a hundred. I bury slightly younger carpenters, stonemasons, shopkeepers, mechanics; members of the VFW, the Lions, the Rotary, the Garden Club, the volunteer fire and rescue squads. I bury a whole generation of housewives whose lives are summed up in the lists of their relatives. Sometimes the survivors consider the scant facts — date of birth and birthplace, parents' and children's names, date and place of death — and find them lacking for a life of eighty-odd years. They add "An avid gardener," or "She loved to cook," "Beloved wife and devoted mother," "Active in the church," or "She was always ready to help those in need."

Her children have not gone off to Yale or Columbia and developed a taste for modern life; they aren't clogging faraway airports at Christmas. They stayed here, married high-school classmates, and became farmers, carpenters, stonemasons, housewives. Over the river and through the woods to grandmother's house is reality here, not nostalgia.

After they've sold off their forefathers' farms to developers, some go west across the mountains, where taxes are lower, but most stay here because it's home. They hang on in the margins, maybe driving east to a construction job but coming back at night, toolboxes rattling in the backs of their trucks, because they can't imagine being happy anywhere else. The idea of loving a *place* seems absurd in America now, a romantic conceit flavored with the last scenes of Scarlett O'Hara, but here it's taken for granted.

Perhaps all the ambitious, wandering genes headed for the cities after the Civil War, leaving only the naturally contented behind. The same surnames run for column after column in our slender phone book and show up on roadside mailboxes all along the lanes: they have looked at the place where they were born and found it good. The mayor and the mail carrier, as well as roads and gravestones and businesses and the dead on the Civil War memorial, all wear the same surnames. The phrase "married into" is still in use: we learn not that Bob married Sally, but that he married into the Reids; she married into the McKimmeys.

Here, an "old family" doesn't imply any sort of distinction. The name doesn't inspire respect, just recognition, and the sense that probably your check won't bounce, because misbehavior would cast a shadow on so many others of the name, alive, dead, and yet unborn.

When I give my own name, I'm usually told that there are Hollands across the mountain; am I connected to them, or perhaps to the Holland who ran for mayor in North Hill some decades ago? I'm not. I am connected to no one in the county and might as well be walking around naked.

Over at the old farmhouse I was introduced to a kid toiling over a balky mower. He shook hands and told me confidently whose boy he was. "I expect you know my parents," he said. I said I hadn't had the pleasure. "My mother's family, then," he insisted, and named them.

"The name sounds familiar," I lied, "but I don't think..."

He looked perfectly astonished. Was I, then, the first person he had met in his whole sixteen years who had met neither his parents nor his grandparents?

On any given day a person in the supermarket could come across his or her entire extended family, one by one, aisle by aisle, pausing to exchange fragments of news among the canned goods. This would horrify city folk, whose relatives tend to get on their nerves, but we're a low-strung lot around here and our satisfaction with our birthplace spreads to include our kin — or perhaps we consider them one and the same. Kin float lightly through the conversations: "My sister was saying, just the other day..."; "My brother-in-law got it in Roanoke"; "I took my aunt Lacy to the bingo at the fire hall Tuesday night."

Relatives are more useful here than in city or suburb. They have tools you can borrow. They're someone to call, in a taxiless world, when you need a ride. Someone to leave the kids with or go hunting with; someone to help get your firewood in or your boat painted. Someone to carry your coffin. From cradle to grave, my neighbors here swing in a hammock of family ties and nobody leaves except for the churchyard. Even the few who fled to Florida get carried home in the end.

Most Americans have traded their relatives for mobility. Families are gum on our shoes; the times call for nimbleness. Decades go by when we don't call our cousins or see our faraway brothers and sisters. The American family so praised by politicians is a mother and father and a minor child or two, a unit too small and temporary to resist centrifugal forces; a single death, a divorce, or just the child driving west in a U-Haul, and the family dissolves without leaving a trace. The new family has the strength and durability of a cabbage moth. (A cynic might suppose our politicians love this little trio not for any pleasure it brings those involved, but because it means the child's father has married the child's mother and between them they, not the state, will feed the child.)

Families depended on the ability to stand still.

In civilized areas people tend, when they mention them at all, to complain about their relatives, but somehow here

· · · · · ·

nobody does, not even those whose mother-in-law came for Christmas and stayed forever.

Complaints of any kind are rare here. Even the most outrageous weather is good for a laugh and a head shake of astonishment: What *will* that old weather think of next?

The new people complain, the people in the new housing developments on the eastern edge of the county. They form citizens' associations for the sole purpose of complaining, and each group spawns task forces and ad hoc committees. They complain about each other's lawns and Christmas decorations, and control them through subcommittees, passing laws against nonconformity. They confront the board of supervisors and write furiously to the newspaper about snakes, snow removal, intersections, police protection, and the insufferable racket of a farmer's corn dryer running through the night at harvesttime. They complain about our famous local turkey buzzards that might well swoop down and carry off their children, and about raccoons that might well be rabid. Because they commute, unencumbered driving is their most basic civil right; they demand new laws banishing farm machinery from the public roads.

But out here to the west in the still-rural hills and towns, the gene for contentment that kept us here keeps us easygoing. The weather could have been worse. Even our mother-in-law could be worse; in fact, since she grew on the same tree, she's probably pretty easy herself and helps out at canning time.

Each town and village and cluster of farms in the county contributes a weekly column to the newspaper. In the eastern housing developments the citizens are restless; they move in

. . . . . .

and move on unremarked; names rarely appear in those columns, which are computer generated and sent in by fax. In the western villages, everyone's noticed, by typewriter or ballpoint, and the columns are often delivered by hand. Every local child who wins a classroom spelling bee is duly celebrated in print. Hosannas greeted the minister's wife when she made a clean blue-ribbon sweep of all three categories, apple, cherry, and "other," in the pie-baking contest at the fair. When a house changes hands, it's news. It becomes a matter of public record that Bill and Betty will be sadly missed, but Joe and Millie and Teresa, age four; Michael ("Micky"), age seven; and Bumps their black Labrador are welcome new neighbors, and Millie enjoys gardening.

Last summer, a man in one of the villages up the road sold the house in which he'd been born and lived for eighty-one years, and bought and moved into the house next door. A friend of mine asked him why. The fellow said, poker-faced, "I reckon it's just the gypsy in me."

Typing obituaries, listing relatives, I can't help feeling slightly superior. It's so un-American, so unadventurous, this contentment, generation after generation settled in the same county, sometimes in the same house, never to set forth over the hills to seek their fortunes in the great wide world.

And sometimes, in certain weathers, I would trade everything I own for that elusive gene.

AS THE EASTERN SUBURBS GROW, I bury more of their denizens. They don't seem to have the staying power of the old families here in the west and many peg out in their forties and fifties. The funeral home rarely tells me why.

. . . . . .

Loneliness? Boredom? Stress? Here in the west, folks would be ashamed to give out before their eighties.

Every few months an important man dies, a man who has come from many faraway places to retire in our countryside. The funeral home sends me his résumé, often several pages long. It doesn't say who his parents were or where he went to church, but it lists his every promotion and accomplishment. He was district manager in Cleveland, then transferred to Dallas where he was regional manager. He sat on boards; chaired conferences; was recognized; received awards. The survivors live in half-a-dozen different states. No pallbearers are mentioned.

I shoehorn him onto the page among farmers and housewives, and he seems to me as lonely as a cowbird's fledgling hatched in a nestful of wrens. But then, I, too, am a cowbird here.

ON FRIDAYS, my duties at the paper include some copyediting, boiling down local press releases on village fairs and pancake breakfasts, and writing up the "years ago" column, staple of all proper country weeklies. I haul down the archives and search out tidbits from ten years ago (more housing developments and a shopping mall sprouting in the eastern half of the county), twenty-five years ago (the first housing development in the eastern county), and fifty years ago (droughts and wheat and the milk production of prize-winning holsteins).

I check the spelling on engagements and weddings. If the least bridesmaid's name is wrong, indignant visitors and phone calls will let me know, and we'll have to run it again, correctly, so that extra copies of the paper can be bought and the piece scissored out and saved in scrapbooks by family, neighbors, and friends. We are the paper of record and each citizen's steps from hospital delivery room to cemetery must be accurately reported.

Trivial work from a reporter's point of view, but I am producing family heirlooms here. A woman called and asked if we would mail her sixteen copies of the current issue with the report of her wedding in it. I thought of this massive bundle of newsprint leaking colored advertising inserts and suggested she take the clipping she already had to the nearest library or copy shop and make her own copies. No, she wanted the newspaper. But the copies would be on better paper, I argued. They'd look cleaner and sharper and last longer, and cost ten cents apiece instead of fifty cents plus postage.

No. She needed the originals. She seemed to feel there'd be something morally shoddy about copies, mere secondhand forgeries of this solemn document, that might cast a shadow over her marriage. Defeated, I routed her call back up to the front desk and returned to my task, freshly awed by my responsibilities.

No one not a resident, or related to one, can be married or buried in our pages for any price. We accept no news of the outside world; no wire service crosses our threshold, nor do our reporters and photographers set foot over the county line in any direction. The courthouse is across the street from the newspaper offices, and on the rare occasions when something illegal has happened, our underemployed cops-and-courts reporter strolls over to ask about it. Mostly it's nothing

. . . . . .

much. For us who work here, happenings even sixty miles away in Washington feel smudged and misty and possibly imaginary.

I SCROUNGED THIS RAGBAG JOB in my struggle to come to terms with being in this place, trying to understand where I was and why I was living alone on a mountain in my middle age, without friends or family or proper employment, surrounded by this mysterious way of life.

I wasn't completely a stranger, at least not to the mountain. When I was a child, a schoolteacher friend of my mother's summered in a pre–Civil War cabin just down the hill from here. She had a son my age, an only child and easily bored, and I was sent to the mountain every summer to keep him company.

The cabin had no running water, no phone, no electricity. In the mornings we children hauled buckets of water from a spring fifty yards from the house, sometimes surprising a thirsty copperhead. The water was heated on a kerosene stove — in damp weather the whole house smelled of kerosene — and we washed the dishes in spattered-blue enamel dishpans. We washed the sooty lamp chimneys from the night before, working our stubby little hands inside their fluted tops. We threw the dishwater out the back door, where earlier we had spat after brushing our teeth.

We were given pails of vegetable peelings and sent across the pasture to the farm to feed the rabbits, the farmer being notoriously lax with his livestock. The gates sagged on their hinges and yielded reluctantly to our shoulders. The pasture contained two inoffensive cows; sometimes goats or sheep, depending on the farmer's whims; and a pair of cart horses,

· · · · · ·

retired except for plowing the garden in the spring. They were white, the fly-specked, yellowish white of retired cart horses. The larger one, Beauty, was indifferent to humans, but Lady, the smaller, hated them. If she spotted me and Alfred from the farthest corner of the field she laid her ears back into a snake's head and bared her slanty tombstone teeth and charged, chasing us to the nearest fence or climbable tree. She was very old, past thirty, they said, but she could put on a surprising turn of speed. I expect we were the bright spot in her day.

In August we hoed between the claustrophobic corn rows higher than our heads. At night we took a flashlight and went down the hill to the outhouse, delicately called "Down-the-Hill," and sat side by side on the smooth board bench shining the light around the crusted, cobwebby walls and frightening each other with the inexplicable noises of a country night. We slept on wire cots in what had once been the chicken house. Things snuffled around in the dark outside.

My mother admired the mountain but saw no reason to suffer needlessly. In 1959 she had an unexpected success with a book and bought a chunk of land uphill from her friend and built a little house, to be a summer retreat where she would write and hide out from her family. She installed a flush toilet, an electric stove, and a phone.

Time passed. I moved to Philadelphia. I had three children of my own, and every August I brought them to the mountain, took their city clothes off, and parked them on the lawn with a trickling hose and some saucepans and water pistols. Summers went by and they grew taller, poked around in the woods, captured toads and turtles, invented elaborate secret games, built things with sticks, and moved through the long, interior process of growing that seems now to have given way to electronics and organized sports.

A summer house is different from the place where you live and work. A summer house is expected to be cut off from social context, isolated from the daily lives of those around it. Summer people everywhere are the objects of derision from natives, as the natives are a mystery to the visitors. Coming here on vacation, we stopped at the nearest town with a supermarket and filled the car with groceries. We bought a peck of peaches at the orchard and drove on up the mountain and stayed here until it was time to go home.

The mountain isn't very high, but being here is like living in a fourth-floor walk-up. Once you're here, you tend to stay here. As summer people, our closest encounter with neighbors was when the grown-ups gathered on the deck at cocktail time and gazed down into the valley at cows lining up to pick their way, with the curiously fastidious gait of cows, back to the barn to be milked. When the right air currents floated up the mountainside we could hear their deep, serious voices.

Sometimes, if we woke up before dawn and went to get a drink of water, we could see lights on down there in the dairy barn: the farmer was milking. We knew his name from his mailbox out by the road, but otherwise we considered him scenery.

More time passed. I wrote magazine articles and an occasional book and worked in a small advertising agency in Philadelphia, where the routines and even the crises had come to seem as familiar to me as my own hands. I rented a three-room house in the heart of the city, walked to work, visited friends. In the usual way of things, my children grew up and my mother died. She left me the little house on the mountain in the far northern corner of Virginia.

I couldn't afford to go on paying rent in Philadelphia and pay taxes and upkeep on a house four hours away. I couldn't sell the place. At the time, nobody was buying any houses anywhere, at any price, and certainly nobody would ever want a one-bedroom, one-bath house without furnace or insulation on ten acres of overgrown woods in the Blue Ridge Mountains.

I quit my job and gave my landlord notice. I kissed my children and friends good-bye and stuffed my possessions into a U-Haul. It was April first, April Fool's Day. Quite a lot of snow still lay on the mountain and a thick freezing fog blotted out the valley and the world beyond. Friends had come with me to help, but the next day they went away. I cried for a while from sheer apprehension, but my small Siamese cat Morgan was well pleased. Even snow-covered woods were better than city windowsills.

As unobtrusively as possible, I worked myself in around my mother's cotton dresses, her mismatched dishes, her books, and the kind of battered silverware and lopsided furniture that finds its way to summer houses. It was hard to move anything to make room for my own things. In a summer house, nothing gets moved or replaced, and when an object, any object, a lithograph of a bird or the Peter Rabbit cup and saucer on the shelf by the phone, has been in the same spot for thirty years, the whole room shrieks with disharmony when it moves. Once a month or so I made a small change, apologizing to the premises. For a long time I lived half in, half out of the house, as if I'd put only one leg in my pants.

Much of the stuff in the house had outlived itself, and came from yard sales to begin with, but it was Mother's, and her ashes have been scattered under the biggest oak tree with a clear view into the windows. This was Mother's sanctuary, and while her children were accepted as summer visitors, she was severe on those who interfered with her arrangements. Besides, throwing anything away here involves a long journey to the dump. My mother and I, between us, have far too many saucepans and scrawny twin bedsheets. Her bookshelves were tightly wedged with books, and for the first week I scrambled like a goat over cartons of my own books until finally I called a man who advertised, on the post-office bulletin board, light hauling.

Frantically, almost at random, I scooped up books to send to the dump. My books, Mother's books, books abandoned by summer visitors, paperback murder mysteries, Edith Wharton, Louisa May Alcott, the Bobbsey Twins, whatever. The light hauler, a fatherly looking black man, opened a few at random and said reproachfully, "Must be a lot of good reading here." There was, of course, and I felt wicked but desperate: I cannot build another whole house for books.

Ever since, I've been groping through the shelves looking for the ghosts of books I threw away.

I TURNED MY ATTENTION to the outdoors, clearing brush in the jungle around the house, a project that was to occupy my spare time for years and yield only the most fleeting results. When you chop down brush, it grows right back again; when you poison it with herbicides, new brush grows in its place. Scatter wildflower seeds, and the wildflowers bloom and the brambles grow up and flourish among them.

My own children's water pistols and comic books kept turning up. It was very quiet.

The valley was still beautiful, with the kind of useful beauty more eloquent to easterners than western canyons and waterfalls. It's impossible to describe a landscape or explain its comeliness, but everyone from the earliest explorers — on horseback because the falls of the Potomac blocked their boats — called this place beautiful. Maybe it has to do with rightness; no artist would alter the placement of a hill here or the bend of a creek; everything is exactly where it belongs, placed here on God's best day. If it's not too fanciful a thought, the land looks happy, as if it were secretly humming to itself under its covers of alfalfa and soybeans. It's been well loved. Our county farmers were the first to sweeten their fields by rotating crops, by sowing lime, gypsum, plaster of paris over clover in their fields to refresh them. As the idea spread, it was named after the county, and farmers stopped exhausting their land and wandering on west and stayed put.

Here still are the rounded pastures for growing meat and milk, fields for growing corn and timothy and soybeans, with barns and silos for storing them. Orchards on a hillside, so the spring frosts can slide down away from their blossoms. Patches of forest for stovewood. Sturdy houses with red tin roofs for families, plain on the farms and dwarfed by barns, gingerbreaded in the towns, all with porches from before the days of air-conditioning. Houses innocent of architects and unwarped by ready-made parts, built by carpenters and stone-masons with an organic rightness the race seems to have forgotten, each window the perfect size and shape, each house unique but obviously kin to the others. My mother used to say that nobody here could build an ugly house because nobody had ever yet seen an ugly house.

Six years ago, when I first moved here, nothing was out of place. I drove all over the western valley and saw nothing to outrage the eye. It helped to soothe the strangeness of being here.

I suppose most of us spend so much time among visual outrages that we've had to blunt our eyes to them, drive around blind. It's a luxury when it's a pleasure to look.

The farm ponds I remembered seemed fewer; they were for livestock in the summer and ice-skating in the winter, and people keep less livestock now and probably ice-skate less. The cows in the field down below were gone, sold off by the farmer's sons when the farmer retired. The roosters that used to crow erratically all day were silenced. The pasture where Lady chased us had grown up in saplings and brush; the farmhouse was occasionally sublet but often empty; its roof sagged. Only a handful of apple trees, descendants of orchard days, still bloomed in the woods, struggling up toward the light. The cabin had been neatly sealed against the weather in case it might be needed again.

The silence was broken only by birdsong in daylight and occasional snuffling by night that sent Morgan to perch alertly on windowsills, a black outline against the moonlight.

There was no one to talk to, no one who would even hear if I screamed. Possibly no one else at all, anywhere. I had been ripped out of context and the torn edges continued to drip blood, slowly, for months.

I started dreaming parties. Two or three times a week my sleep would be filled with faces and voices, laughing and

chatting. They were wonderful parties and everyone came —
my mother, my ex-boss's wife, Eleanor Roosevelt, Humphrey
Bogart, and all the friends I'd left behind. I woke up in the
morning cheered and refreshed by all that merrymaking.
Then, as abruptly as they'd started, the parties stopped. Perhaps my subconscious was forgetting faces.

In the beginning friends would call from Philadelphia, asking me when I was coming back. Then they gave up and
stopped calling. The phone sat dumb as a candlestick and
when it did ring, I jumped and dropped things. I hated to
call and report myself in to friends and relations because I
had nothing to report. I wrote, and consigned my manuscripts
to the mail, and sometimes, soundlessly, an answering letter
or check would appear in the mailbox up on the county road.

I HAVE READ earnest books by people who set forth
deliberately to be alone for some days or even weeks in order
to find spiritual fulfillment and uncover the nature of their
true selves. I admire these seekers, but either I'm hopelessly
shallow and have no spiritual self to be revealed, or else these
excursions into solitude need to be voluntary to produce. I
paced the floor and muttered to myself. Talked to the cat.
Took up cigarettes again. Wrote scathing letters to newspaper
and magazine editors at night and tore them up in the morning. All I learned about my inner self was that I was less brave,
less capable, and less self-sufficient than I'd liked to think.
Standing on the ladder cleaning gutters I thought, *If I fall,
how badly will I be hurt? Will I be able to drive myself thirty
miles to the hospital? Or will I hit my head on that rock and
lie here forever?* Suppose I got sick; what happens to people
here too sick to go buy groceries and fill prescriptions?

Six years ago the only human habitation in sight was a tidy little farm in the valley, on Yellow Schoolhouse Road. I could see it clearly with binoculars from the deck. I didn't know who lived there, but it was comforting to see.

Sometimes, just as I was beginning to relax, the precarious mountain electric power would go off, reminding me of just how helpless I really was.

I DROVE DOWN THE MOUNTAIN, peering into the woods for lights. The power had been out all afternoon and I'd been trying to work in the mournful shadows of candle-light, in the deepening chill, my house lying dead around me: no light, no heat, no water. No stove, refrigerator, computer, and only the single flush left in the toilet tank. Without electricity I wallowed rudderless as a raft at the world's end, striving only to keep the pipes from freezing, a woman too lone and helpless to maintain her own generator as proper montagnards do. The powerless cabin down the hill, in my childhood, was inconvenient, but it didn't feel for-lorn — how can a house miss what it has never known? My mother's house runs on electricity and, without it, stands still.

By the time the power crew came, cheerful in yellow slickers, headlights blazing as they hacked their way toward the power pole, I was ready to cry. I was ready to move to a city, any city, where toilets always flush and nobody needs to be manly.

I got in my car and fled.

Down at the Gap I turned west, and there in the dark forest below the highway, over toward the West Virginia border, gleamed the authentic twinkle of electricity. I plunged down the switchbacked road like a diver and found, on a hairpin turn, a nameless building with beer neon in the windows and a parking lot full of pickups. I skidded onto the gravel, jumped out and, mindless as a moth, barged through the lighted doorway.

And stopped. All eyes, to put it mildly, were on me. Was I the first stranger ever to cross that threshold? Certainly I was the first woman ever to walk in unescorted. I can't say a silence fell, because a football game yammered from the television on the wall, but it *looked* like a silence. Eight or ten men between the ages of forty and eighty sat at four tables pushed together; pairs of younger people sat at single tables. All wore down vests and jeans (at least I was dressed to match) and all the men wore caps, frontward or backward. No one sat at the bar except a Doberman on the end stool. Everyone except the Doberman stared.

Could I pretend to be lost; ask directions? No, who would get lost by turning off a four-lane highway to burrow down this tiny road?

Out from the kitchen came the proprietress, and she was not dressed to match. As if costumed for some private Halloween party, she wore a fringed white leather jacket, white leather miniskirt, and white cowboy boots, and she bustled — if you can bustle in a miniskirt — kindly over to me, the stranger.

I blurted, "The power's off on the mountain. I saw your lights."

"You come sit right here at the bar," she said consolingly. "Don't mind Max, he's real gentle, he's just waiting for his beer. Now what can I get you? Hamburger, cheeseburger, Bud or Miller Lite?"

. . . . . .

"Bud, I guess."

She cracked one expertly and then paused, holding the bottle. "Do you want a glass?"

I glanced around at the tables. Eighteen or twenty beer bottles were in sight but no glasses. Through the kitchen door I could see grill and fryer and paper plates, but no place to keep a glass.

"I can *get* you a glass," she insisted warmly.

Did she keep one hidden under the counter? Or was she offering to jump in her pickup and drive home for one? Bring it to comfort me, a beer glass for the orphan of the power outage? I blinked back tears of gratitude. "Bottle's fine," I said.

She set it down and brought an open bottle from the shelf and splashed beer into Max's saucer. He leaned decorously between his paws to lap it, and I lifted my own in my fist and swigged. The room's conversations resumed.

I drank slowly, dawdling to soak in light. Replete, Max sighed and pillowed his head on his paws on the bar. When the bottle was empty, I paid, being careful not to overtip too gratefully, and went home.

The yellow-slickered crew was gone and the house was a living hymn to electricity. The lights blazed; the refrigerator moaned; the heaters ticked and purred; the wall clock, five hours late, buzzed; and the VCR flashed 12:00! 12:00! 12:00! like a silent rooster crowing.

Life is different here. In civilized areas you can usually count on civilization — snowplows, electricity, the Yellow Pages — while hereabouts we have to depend on the support of various angels. Angels in yellow slickers. Angels in white leather miniskirts. I only pray they come when called.

———

. . . . .

I DO HAVE NEIGHBORS. Less than a mile away but out of sight at the end of the twisting dirt lane live C. J., his wife, and their two granddaughters. Sometimes we meet, usually in our cars.

MY CAR WALLOPS into the ruts and scratches through the blackberries in the lane. ("This mess has *got* to be cut back," I mutter, deftly putting it in the passive voice to avoid responsibility.) Around the bend at the big rock, I encounter C. J. in his car. Each of us makes a quick calculation: Who's closer to a pullout? I am. Slowly, lurching in and out of blackberries, I back up to the half-moon kept cleared for this purpose and swerve into it. C. J. follows me, pulls alongside, stops, and rolls down his window. I roll down mine; to wave and drive on would be rude, so rude that our dusty country cars would probably be shocked into stalling. "Isn't this grand weather we've been having?" he says. "Almost feels like spring."

In the city, people use the phone or run into each other on street corners and chat. In the suburbs, they chat over coffee at the kitchen table or from backyard to backyard, hedge clippers or charcoal lighter in hand. Down in the valley, everyone stops to chat with everyone else, everywhere they go. On the mountain we talk in our cars, engines idling. Sometimes two pickups, nose to tail, block traffic on the county road while their drivers chat.

Behind the wheel C. J. simply feels more like chatting. Cars melt the social reserve — not to say crustiness — common to mountain folk the world over; the naturally gregarious don't choose to live on isolated homesteads in the hills. On our own front porches, we're territorial and eye the approaching guest with suspicion, if not an actual shotgun, but the car is a kind of moving demilitarized zone.

It's also our best friend, every countryperson's cherished helpmeet, staff of life, most necessary companion. Without it, we'd be as helpless as a tortoise on its back. Most households have several, maybe a comfortable sedan for church, a pickup for hauling wood or slain deer, and a battered generic vehicle considered dispensable, for trips of dubious safety. On the mountain, at least, one has four-wheel drive for winter. The nearest public transportation is fifty miles away; the post office is a fourteen-mile round-trip; basic groceries, twenty. "Get a neighbor to drive you" is easily said in the suburbs, but here it's a major request, to be saved against the day we make a mistake with the chain saw.

Residents of a mountainous neighboring state are derisively accused of decorating their lawns with the ghosts of transportation past, skeletal Fords and Chevys nested in weeds, with vines and wrens' nests where their windshields used to be. Maybe, though, this is as much sentiment as slovenry; maybe after all those faithful years, the owners couldn't bear to send them to the compactor and turned them out to grass instead.

Securely cradled in the laps of our loyal cars, we lighten up, lower our guard, chat with our neighbors.

The next time I meet C. J. we're up by the mailboxes. This time we have more on our minds than weather. Someone has bought ten landlocked acres down on the spur of the mountain; the resulting cat's cradle of rights-of-way involves us all, and the footprint of the newcomer rouses our territoriality. This time, C. J. turns off his engine. I turn off mine — again, it would be unthinkable to go on impatiently idling when the other has signified, by the turn of his key, that he has some-

22 *Coming from Away*

thing important to say. This time, because it's so substantive, C. J. gets out of his car and curves over to lean on my opened window.

This is a very particular country posture, a signature stance as definitive as the cowboy's bowlegged slouch. I understand that once, back in history, it was a different position, with one foot up on the running board as if to keep the car from bolting, but now, without running boards, we lean on the window. Tall people talking into small cars might be more comfortable resting their arms on the roof, but this would be too assertive, too invasive, so they crouch instead.

Of course, we could have used the phone. Or arranged to meet over a kitchen table. But no, we waited until, in the natural course of things, our cars met up.

In a way, this car talk is the perfect social occasion. It's spontaneous; accidental, in fact. It's voluntary. It takes place on neutral, nonterritorial ground, yet safely within our loved and trusted private property. And when we've chatted enough, we can drive off with a honk and a wave, refreshed by human contact, back to our secret fortresses in the hills.

To THE VALLEY FOLK, the hills themselves seem like secret fortresses. In all times and places even mountains that never spew lava or rain down rocks have felt remote and possibly hostile to those below. Maidens have been sacrificed on specially built altars up at the crest, after which the villagers scurried back down to terra cognita.

I call the refrigerator repairman. Can he come, I ask, and look at my refrigerator?

Of course. No problem. The voice on the phone is cheerful and helpful.

· · · · · ·

Coming from Away 23

When I give the directions, the cheer vanishes. Reluctance drags at the voice. He doesn't know as he could come up on the *mountain*, not just for a little job like that.

But I'm less than two miles from the highway, the main highway he travels every day.

He's unconvinced. "Tell you what. Somebody else calls from up there, and I can do the two jobs together, why, I'll give you a call and come on up. Otherwise . . ."

This is the Blue Ridge, a mountain range that in many western states would hardly qualify as a speed bump, but in the mind it towers like Everest.

The east-west highway crosses the Gap as it has since it was an Indian footpath, and smaller, older cars like mine make toilsome work of it. A Mrs. Browne, traveling by wagon in 1755, wrote that it was "one continuous mountain for three miles," and it is. Still, it's part of the known world; people pass over it without thinking. But if, at the top of the Gap, you turn north or south and continue climbing, you're on what's always called "the mountain." The mountain is different. To be here is to be *up* here.

Friends planning to visit from the north speak of coming "up" to see me; four hours driving south fade to nothing beside the brief climb up the mountain. (They also ask if they can bring me anything, as if I winched my supplies in with a bucket on a rope.) Arriving, they emerge from their cars with triumph on their faces befitting the Iditarod winner: they have come up the mountain. Overnight guests, city folk who scoff at the dangers stalking their own streets, tend to sleep, a bit apologetically, with a sharp or heavy object close by the bed, in case the unknown should seep in through the walls in the night. One stalwart young man found a rusty machete in the toolroom and slept with it under his pillow.

Once here, though, they find it hard to leave and usually stay over Sunday night, not as a tribute to my hospitality but because they feel so perilously remote. The journey back down is not to be undertaken lightly, and certainly not in the dark. Monday morning they pack a Thermos and sandwiches and set forth like Amundsen.

People in the valley towns regard us montagnards with a mix of respect and suspicion. The social bridges between us feel fragile, like Tibetan bridges made of thongs. We're different. Living up here without civilized services, without trash collection, streetlights, sewers, civic water, cable television, or convenience stores, almost without neighbors, we seem scarcely distinguishable from our bears. The county line runs along the ridge so that each of the contiguous jurisdictions feels we belong to the other, and no sheriff's car patrols the ridge road to check on our speed or our seat belts. In spring and fall a dense woolly fog settles over the ridge and hides it from the flatlands below like a door closing over secrets.

"It's beautiful up there," people say, but they might be talking about the rings of Saturn — hardly a place to set up housekeeping.

The gulf between us widens. Nobody will ever bring a fiber-optic cable here to carry us into the new world of interactive communications that, I'm told, will change the way everyone else lives. We will never even get CNN. We will grow ever stranger, more foreign as the years pass, and not even the rapacious housing developers will brave the climb.

In the ancestral memories of valley folk, the valley was the respectable, hardworking place to live, the good flat land for cows and corn and wheat. The mountain was where you went to hunt squirrel and deer in the fall, but its scattered residents were renegades who probably never came down for church on Sundays. Their morals escaped supervision. They didn't need to bathe or shave or watch their language. Their children probably ran wild as bobcats and never went to school.

Exploring in the woods, I've stumbled on the ruined foundations of their cabins, with blackened rocks where the fireplace was. Nearby there's always a small trash pile; anything decomposable has decomposed, but the bottles remain. Medicine bottles, dozens, hundreds of them, small and narrow and delicately shaped, often in a faded bluish green color. They mean a woman lived here. Women of any respectability couldn't join their husbands in the consolations of moonshine and so fell back on medicine, probably mostly alcohol, maybe laced with opiates, to soothe the nerves rubbed raw by loneliness. I stand there holding a small dirt-caked bottle in each hand, surrounded by the litter of fallen chimney stones. By the open hole of the root cellar, she planted the common orange wild daylilies; they're still here. Daylilies never leave their homes.

Sister, I think.

No doubt valley people always told stories about mountain people that would make your hair stand on end. No doubt some of them were true. Sometimes I hear, "Uncle of mine used to live on the mountain," and I can tell by the reflective tone that this uncle wasn't reliably housebroken. The kind of uncle you're obliged to invite to family weddings but keep your fingers crossed hoping he won't come, hoping the mailman won't be able to find him. An uncle whose diet was heavy on squirrel and rabbit and who probably ran a still — for generations moonshine was the mountain's principal cash crop, revenuers and deputy sheriffs being no more eager than refrigerator repairmen to venture up into the unknown.

Then there was the plane crash, lingering ominously in valley memory. Nobody's forgotten the crash, and when someone wants to place me, he asks which side of the crash I'm on. I've learned to say, "About two miles to the north," and he nods and knows where I live.

It happened December 1, 1974, and as its anniversaries roll by, conversation still comes back to circle around it. A Boeing 727 out of Indianapolis, headed for Dulles Airport in an easterly storm, slammed into the mountain at well over two hundred miles an hour with ninety-two people aboard. All able-bodied men, in the quaint old phrase that still lays obligations here, turned out to help and lived on for decades with their nightmares roiled. They came to look for survivors. They peered around through the fog and then put the first-aid kits back in their pickups and collected body bags instead.

It was *Macbeth*, or *King Lear*, or Judgment Day. Thick fog streamed in the wind, mixed with freezing rain. Power saws roared to clear the road. To the west, trees had been sheared off for three hundred yards and to the east, at the rock ledge, flames flared for hours through the fog like hell itself. The men fanned out to search among the scraps of wreckage for whatever could be found. One volunteer told a reporter, "If I could understand what I'm standing in the middle of, I'd really get sick."

"*I* was sick," a barrel-chested man on a barstool told me

twenty years later. "I just kept throwing up until finally I quit and went home. Not like we were going to find anything worth saving anyway."

The blond who now washes my hair at the beauty parlor had to ask to be relieved. She'd been directing volunteers for three hours before she said, "I'll do anything else, I'll park cars, anything, only I can't stay here any more." After that they put everyone on shorter shifts, rotating the horror.

Night came and the rain turned to sleet, weirdly lit by lightning bolts striking here and there on the mountain. Big Mike remembers a ball of St. Elmo's fire. The volunteers slogged on, soaked and freezing. Womenfolk supplied gallons of hot coffee. By the next morning, the remains of the ninety-two had been gathered into two hundred body bags and stashed in the village community center, formerly the elementary school, for assembly and possible identification.

There'd already been two recent crashes along the ridge; in one of them, eight bodies were too finely splintered to identify and had to be buried at public expense. But it was the great crash, the 727, that lives on as binding common mythology here. In a more civilized area, only the professionals would remember, the fire and medical workers paid to handle disasters, professionally detached, doling out sanitized reports to the public; but here in volunteer country, it was everyone's disaster, everyone's long bad dream.

The spring after the crash, on a visit, I drove up and saw the trees sheared off, all at the same height as if by the lawnmower of the gods, and the hillside littered with scraps of clothing from the luggage ripped open in the plane's belly.

The forest healed its wounds a long time ago and no stranger now would be able to say where the plane crashed,

. . . . . .

but every native could show you exactly. When I say I'm two miles north, they could find me in their sleep.

The recording boxes held no explanation. There never was any explanation. After the investigation, the official reports were vague and meaningless. It was as if the mountain itself had roused from its brooding slumber in a sudden rage of weather and snatched down a plane and smashed it to pieces.

Those ghosts are still young yet, but there must be layers of older ones, and older mountain legends and superstitions that nobody's told me or, more likely, superstitions forgotten for a hundred years and lingering only as uneasiness. This ridge is the oldest mountain chain in the world. In all those eons, it must have gathered spirits more sinister than the gray shadows of Mosby's Rangers still celebrating the Civil War.

I'd ask a Manahoac, if there were any of those nomadic hunters left. Over this way in 1608, Captain John Smith caught a Manahoac named Amoroleck, who told him, he wrote, that "they had heard we were a people come from under the world to take their world from them." Nobody knows where the Manahoac went, but the buffalo that used to be thick here were gone by 1730; perhaps the first Indians went looking for them. Later the Susquehannocks, called by white settlers "the most noble and heroic nation of Indians," came and died of our smallpox.

When Alfred and I were children on the mountain, we carried Indian arrowheads around in our pockets. Spring plowing turned up shards and axheads. Over in the valley, near the river, people have found bits and pieces from the Early Archaic Period, 8000–6000 B.C., and an arrowhead thought to have been used against the woolly mammoth.

. . . . . .

None of this makes me feel more at home here, floating loose among the millennia.

I remember vaguely, and look up, the words of Seathl, the chief of the Duwamish, when he signed over his people's lands in Washington State. He said, "When your children's children think themselves alone in the field, the store, the stop upon the highway, or in the silence of the pathless woods, they will not be alone.... At night when the streets of your cities and villages are silent and you think them deserted, they will throng with the returning hosts that once filled them and still love this beautiful land. The White Man will never be alone."

Somehow this isn't as comforting as it might be.

THE OTHER NIGHT I got up at three in the morning to let a cat in. A heavy snow had just started to melt and in the moonlight two deer were picking their way across the side yard looking for browse, throwing long shadows. Up behind the house a thumbprint of brilliant light moved silently, flying low and south along the ridge. I hadn't seen one in several years. Most people who watched them here, back when this was a house of many guests and there were more things in the sky to watch, are reluctant to talk about them, since flying objects aren't a respectable thing to see. The other lights, the ones that dance in the summer woods eight to twenty feet off the ground, like softball-sized lightning bugs only whiter and brighter, are less embarrassing. Being apparently terrestrial, they must have some simple chemical explanation.

The flying light slipped out of view in silence and I went back to bed.

· · · · · ·

I NEVER RETURNED to the little bar on the horseshoe bend with the beer-drinking Doberman. That was emergency shelter, and I was made welcome as an orphan of the power failure, but not as a prospective regular. A woman walking in there alone without so much as a flat tire to excuse her, even to order a hamburger at lunchtime, would be unseemly.

Some days I find myself listening for the sound of C. J.'s car crunching gravel, passing through the woods below me. When he remembers, he gives the horn a short, neighborly toot. Some days it sounds like music.

Fireflies find their way into the house and I gather them gently and help them back outside. Lacking people, I find I've grown more solicitous of even quite small beetles trapped in the bathtub, and downright motherly with moths, spiders, and crickets.

I cling to my twice-weekly stints at the newspaper, nourished by the backs of people's heads bent over their keyboards and the sound of ringing phones. The police scanner natters on rather peaceably, mostly about people who are having trouble breathing and small children accidentally locked in cars. Scrap by scrap, I am let into the paper's traditions and the peculiarities of bygone editors. People offer me treasured misprints and headlines — "You Can Put Pickles Up Yourself!" — but I am only part-time here, and I'm older than the rest of the newsroom; the pay is terrible and the jobs function as a kind of postgraduate course for the very young.

I drive the valley's wandering gravel roads and stop at all the tiny fairs in crossroads villages, pretend an interest in the crafts and needlework and the winners of the watermelon-seed-spitting contest, and inhale the smoke from the barbecue pit. Then I drive home up the mountain. Where can a person unattached, without family, poke her nose in here? Everywhere I go, everyone is friendly and cheerful, but I slide off the local world like a drop of oil.

I see men in pairs and groups, women in pairs and groups, families pulling up extra chairs in the restaurant. Everyone is far too polite to stare at me standing alone at the fair or eating alone in the diner, but self-consciously I can feel them noticing. In cities, nobody notices.

The only other single people here are widows in their eighties, and I've signed up for riverboat trips and museum tours with them, but they doze off on my shoulder in the van and when roused and spoken to they search my face in alarm and confusion. Well, bless them; there I, too, shall walk.

The sexes don't mingle casually here. In the North Hill diner most booths and tables are open to anyone, but at the back, as in all proper diners, two tables are permanently pushed together for the local men. It's occupied from six in the morning until after lunch by a rotating population. After a while I come to recognize their faces, these regulars. No woman sits there, ever. Should one of the regulars bring his wife in for lunch, they sit in the neighboring booth and the man takes part in the men's-table chat from this decent distance.

Down at the tavern, men sit at the bar. A man who has brought his wife will sit at the nearest table and shout comments to his cronies across her shoulder.

The separation of men and women seems to make for healthy marriages; marriage doesn't get leaned on too hard. Husband and wife don't expect to draw all their social nourishment from each other. Women visit with their mothers and aunts and sisters; men go fishing with their brothers-in-law. I suppose the custom's left over from farming days, when men worked with other men producing the cash crop, and women, alone or together, produced the food for the family and hired hands. Chickens and eggs were the woman's work, and the family cow, and vegetables canned and pickled. An industrious woman could make a good thing of her egg money, saving it up in a Mason jar; egg money was sacredly hers to spend. As a partnership, the lines were clear: no woman worked in the fields; no man fed chickens.

Today, no man changes diapers, but no woman changes tires. A woman with a flat tire stands by the side of the highway and waits for a passing man to pull over. One always does.

The men serve together at the volunteer fire and rescue squads and talk to each other at the diner and the tavern. The women are in charge of schools and charity and church.

I have no children or grandchildren in school, an abnormal condition here. Much of a woman's life revolves around the schools and their seasons; most of the programs at the community centers are for preschool children; local fairs promise games for children of all ages, face painting, and a clown. (It's always the same clown, with the same strained and raggedy repertoire, but novelty around here is less compelling than tradition.)

Women volunteer everywhere. They drive meals to the elderly, shelve books at the library, teach Sunday school, and answer the phone at the fire and rescue. I know I should sign on to do something useful, but back where I came from, volunteers were a closed circle of the socially important and the socially striving, and their labors consisted of organizing expensive fund-raising balls for themselves and their friends.

· · · · · ·

Coming from Away 33

It's different here, where volunteers get sweaty and dirty and shoulder much of the daily work of the western half of the county, but in the back of my mind, unpaid labor still seems frivolous, and my unreliability in winter would make me more nuisance than asset to any institution.

That leaves church. Sunday supplies our heaviest morning rush hour, and at every church flocks of families pile out of their cars at the same moment and wave to each other. White people now wear borderline-casual clothes, but blacks still dress and set aside a spring Sunday when all the women wear their most elegant hats. Morning services spill over into afternoon potluck dinners, choir practice, bus trips to ice-cream socials at other churches.

Tentatively, carefully dressed, I tiptoe into a pretty carpenter's-gothic church with gingerbreading and a tall pointy steeple. Immediately all eyes are upon me: a stranger. Church here is an extension of family. In fact, they call themselves family, as in newspaper notices announcing "The pastor of Mt. Olivet and his church family will be the guests at North Hill United Methodist...."

There's no way to start off gradually, slip in unnoticed, and sit at the back. I am greeted and welcomed and questioned. I feel hideously awkward, as if I'd burst into a stranger's house during a birthday party and everyone pressed me to stay for cookies and punch. And as in the fairy tales, once I bit into a cookie, I'd be theirs forever. Once adopted I'd be committed, probably unto the very grave. All my city instincts bristle, and I button my privacy up to my throat and back off politely, leaving the ninety and nine in the fold.

With neither child nor church, I have no door to slip through into living here.

. . . . . .

Late one afternoon, after a day when C. J.'s car was never heard down on the lane, I drive down to the tavern in the next town beyond North Hill. This is a respectable restaurant where beer is routinely served in glasses; perhaps I won't be too conspicuous. I'll have a drink in public, eat something, eavesdrop.

All the tables are filled with early diners. One stool at the bar stands empty, and in desperation I sit on it. It wobbles dangerously. I order a drink.

No one is rude, but I can feel the subterranean shudder. After a silence, the men on either side lean forward to talk to each other across me. The blond barmaid, on the proper side of the bar for a woman, avoids my eyes. I sit up very straight, fiercely projecting that I am not from around here and have no way of knowing the local rules, and that where I come from women, even solitary women, are allowed to sit wherever they please. I look straight ahead at a framed photograph of a fat man in a tin bathtub pouring water from a jug over his head. Over the fireplace the manly visage of Stonewall Jackson gazes sorrowfully at me. Chunks of charred logs breathe out the sourness of fireplaces in summer; apparently the heating system is no more efficient than the air-conditioning is now. The man at the end of the bar cranks open the tiny casement window to let in some air from the field outside and the barmaid turns on the television news.

I make a light comment on the weather report to the man on my left, a burly fellow with a dark-red tan and streaks of sawdust on his battered jeans. Startled, he flicks his eyes at me, jerks his head once in acknowledgment, and turns his shoulder blade toward me.

Three days later I come back. This time the barmaid nods at me.

. . . . . .

Coming from Away 35

For several months I pause on my way home from the newspaper and sit on a barstool at the tavern. I behave myself — except, of course, for the initial gross impropriety of being there at all. Occasionally I toss something into the conversation around me, careful not to frame it as a question that needs answering.

Time passes. I learn the names of the regulars and use them in brief greetings. Eventually they learn my name and where I live, and several begin to greet me when I come in. The barmaid starts to say "The usual?" and later stops asking, pouring it when I open the door.

I go up north for a visit. When I come back after ten days' absence, Big Mike says, "Hey there, stranger, where've you been?"

Gradually the men on their barstools begin to tell me things. They still disapprove, of course, but I come bringing new ears to a place where everyone knows the same stories and shares the same history.

Bill tells me what happened to the movie theater. Once there was a movie theater in this town. I remember passing it when I was a child, though it never occurred to my family, once we were up on the mountain, to come down to the valley and go to a movie. Bill's mother owned and operated it, and she ran a tight ship. Only the nicest movies appeared there, and during them she prowled the aisles with a flashlight checking on the teenaged couples. No necking was allowed, and if she found even an arm laid across the back of the neighboring seat she reached across and tapped it sternly.

The last movie was *The Bad News Bears*. From the title she'd assumed it was cute and suitable. It wasn't. There was language. Bill's mother was stunned that the corruption of the times had spread even to such an apparently innocent subject; she stopped the movie and turned on the houselights. She returned everyone's money and closed the theater forever.

The building still stands, because no building in this town has ever been torn down. Farm machinery, in season, is repaired there now.

I AM STILL AN ABERRATION. Time has passed but no other woman, however well-known and connected, has ever sat at the bar. Only I have managed to claim a stool there where I can look at faces and hear voices after the quiet days.

Perhaps these scraps are all I'll be able to manage here, and sometimes I wonder why I've done such a cross-grained thing to myself. When I decided to come, I didn't seem to have any option. Here was this little house that my mother gave me, and I could hardly abandon it to the wolves and the weather, let its paint peel off in curls and its roof shingles loosen and drop. It was left on the doorstep of my life, and I had to take it in.

Now I need to learn the world that came with it and work toward the grace to be contented here, though I can never really belong. It's not so much coming from away, it's the alien life I brought with me. Comparatively speaking, I am stiff with sophistication. Invisible splints and trusses prevent me from playing bingo, teaching Bible class, or driving down to Harmony United Methodist with a carload of brownies for their bake sale. There's an admission fee to be paid for full membership here, and I came bearing currency from another country.

the day's work

．．．．．．．．．．．．．．．．．

Much of what I think I know I learned from reading books, which aren't always reliable sources, especially on country matters. Books get written by writers, and writers tend to be overeducated and they daydream a lot and can't be trusted. Some books are pure nostalgia, some pure fantasy, and some just old. Country books are chock-full of simple folk straight out of Wordsworth and James Whitcomb Riley who talk funny but stand ever ready to help those more sophisticated with their menial tasks.

I've never actually seen a "hired man," featured player in generations of country memoirs, but I keep looking, with diminishing hopes. I want him. I need him. There he stands in my mind's eye, a man of few words named Lem or Zeke. He drives a battered blue Ford pickup and wears those boots vulgarly named for their ability to kick pasture droppings around. He tends to vanish during game-hunting days and the opening of trout season, then reappear with a nice cut of venison or a couple-three fish for my freezer, by way of compensation. He looks around, spitting reflectively into the weeds, to see what needs doing here. He feels responsible.

This shared responsibility is what I yearn for. I'm sick and tired of being the only person who cares about this place. Oh, I don't mean I can't hire help, *specific* help; the fellow with the hydraulic log splitter to mince my firewood, the one with the giant tiller to plow the garden. They come (except in deer or turkey seasons), they do the job, take their money, and go away until their jobs roll around again. They don't see the larger picture. They don't, get right down to it, *care*.

The hired man of my Wordsworthian dreams cares. He's full of opinions, however wrongheaded, about how much snow we'll have, when to plant peas, and how to cook squirrel. Being local, he still calls the local properties by the names of owners who perished in the recent unfortunate War Between the States, and he'll know a thing or two about what grows well on my side of the mountain and which plumber to call. He'll know the local stories. He'll know the details about the family, long ago, who lived in the cabin of my childhood summers; all I know is that they threw their two sons out of the house for laziness and insubordination, and the sons moved into the crawl space underneath the house and lived there, some say, for years.

And being local and a man, he'll feel free to advise and bully me, me being but a lone woman and an outlander at that: "No'm, Miz Holland, I'm taking down that-there tree before it shades out the berry patch. No call to keep it, t'ain't nothing but a 'fras anyhow."

I have never heard anyone, anywhere, talk like this, but since this is how hired men talk in the memoirs, it's how I'll recognize my hero when we meet.

· · · · · ·

My Lem or Zeke will be a throwback to the days when a man's experience and strength, his judgment and the skill of his hands, were more important than the machinery he could bring to bear on the task. Machinery gave rise to all this feckless specialization: the man who's invested in a heavy-duty brush hog or log splitter wants to go around the county brush hogging and log splitting, earning back his investment, not putting them away to clean my chimney or prune my peach tree. He can clean his own chimney and prune his own peach trees, but it's not worth his while to hire out to do it. Men hereabouts have no sentimental nostalgia about the days of hand labor. They like gas-burning tools, preferably yellow, and the bigger and louder the better. Full-grown dogwoods topple meekly in their paths.

Some years back, a long power outage in the valley sent dairy farmers in pickup trucks scuttling along the back roads looking for senior citizens who remembered how to milk a cow by hand. Now I suppose the few remaining dairies have generators and the hand milkers are free to die off.

The hired man could milk. He was a generalist. Notice how nonspecific his job description; not a gardener or a carpenter or a tree surgeon, simply a man, and hired, who could turn his hand to whatever needed doing. Machinery narrowed the playing field and withered the old, various skills. Of course, it's also done wonders for social status.

The old work took learning and practice. The art of swinging an ax was handed down from elders to twelve-year-olds. Now any country twelve-year-old can run a chain saw and the only skill involved was in raising the money to buy it, but its owner has become an independent contractor, socially far above the hired man, who, however insubordinate, was basically nothing but a salaried employee. Around here, being salaried isn't exactly a *disgrace* — for a woman, it's quite acceptable — but for a man, even a teenaged man, it's nothing to brag about either: Real men don't get paychecks. Salaries imply obedience to a boss, scarcely different from flat-out slavery.

When a man gets work that calls for more than one worker, he scrounges among his acquaintances for someone to help. They work in tandem, as men like to do. I pay the first man, who settles up with the second. Next time their positions may be reversed.

My hired man will be on salary. (Not that I could afford it, but then, I don't see any applicants, either.) This would eliminate the delicate matter of money, of whom to pay and how much and under what circumstances. Apparently there are no fixed rates for jobs. Rates depend. They depend on what else the worker would rather be doing, like fishing; on the weather; on the worthiness of the job; on my personal worthiness. I've already committed the hideous social error of offering to pay for help in an emergency, but how can I identify an emergency? Apparently if I want the luxury of a plowed lane after only six inches of snow, payment is expected. But a couple of feet of snow is a public disaster, a community matter, and plowing me out is a neighborly duty for which the offer of money is an insult.

Shortly after I moved here, I found a wondrously helpful and capable man who came to clear brush. He worked like a dynamo; he worked as if the land and the problem were his own. He cut fallen trees into firewood, stacked it, and burned the slash. He cleared more in a single day than I, flailing around with hand tools, had managed in months. At the end

· · · · · ·

of the day I thanked him effusively. He wiped his brow on his sleeve and looked around, considering. "Next time I come," he said, "I'll do that section down there. You got a lot of leaners there, I'll clear that out. Maybe next week if I can manage it."

My heart leapt with joy. I asked him how much I owed him for today. He named his price, and I was shocked. A high-school kid would make that at McDonald's. "Are you sure?" He was sure.

I wrote him a check, and I added an hour's modest wage to it. He scowled. "That's too much," he said.

Beaming, I said, "That's a bonus for signing on. And doing such a great job."

He folded the check and put it in his pocket. He stowed his chain saw in his pickup and drove away. He never came back. I tried calling, but I got his wife. She said he'd call me, but he never did.

I want a man I can pay by the week, come weal, come woe, no feelings hurt.

I'll need to leapfrog backward in time to find my hired man, my tobacco-spitting jewel, my good right hand. Maybe back before World War II, back before rototillers, back when the tools of life were a hoe, a hammer, and a well-balanced ax. As soon as they solve the problem of time travel that's where I'm going, to return triumphant with a man of few words named Zeke or Lem.

BEING HELPLESS, I took my chain saw to be sharpened at the hardware store. It's a store you might find intact at the Smithsonian, under "Americana." Barrels and bins bulge into the aisles, bicycles and birdhouses hang from the

· · · · · ·

ceiling, shelves bend under hefty enameled kettles, stoneware pickle crocks, and cast-iron muffin pans. In spring, seeds are sold from five-gallon cans that once held kerosene, cans left from the days when kerosene stoves heated the store; the clerk ladles them out in a tin scoop and weighs them on a venerable scale. Behind the counter, reaching to the ceiling and halfway down the store, stands a wall of blackened oak drawers full of small metal objects. Men come in and plunk a small metal object down on the counter, the clerk considers it and then rolls the ladder down a few yards, climbs up, and rummages in a couple of these unmarked drawers, returning triumphant with a duplicate small metal object, related somehow to plumbing or electricity or carpentry.

In the back, paint is mixed according to formulas copied in longhand from a battered loose-leaf binder. At the counter, bills are toted up on an adding machine, then re-added in the clerk's head. Credit cards are suspect; payment here is by personal check or, more usually, from a handwritten bill mailed at the end of the month.

The store belongs, as it has for generations, to a descendant of one of the town's founding fathers and bears his name. So does the store across the street that sells refrigerators. So does the store on Main Street that sells tables and chairs. Everyone knows the family; everyone's kids went to school with their kids. Everyone comes to the hardware store for advice on matters ranging from aphids to woodstoves.

But the store is no longer hardware king in the valley. Just twelve miles away, in the new shopping mall, a hardware store the size of a family farm has appeared, part of a famous chain of hardware stores. I had to go there once, for bear-proof trash cans. Things are cheaper there. And there's room for more

· · · · · ·

The Day's Work 43

things, for lampshades and floor tiles and sinks and toilets, a whole household world. Everything looks bright and clean. Nothing is hidden away in small oak drawers.

Out of loyalty or stubbornness or a natural reluctance to grease the wheels of progress, the natives here still go to this store, with its long and honorable past and brief future. The new people in the new suburbs go to the new store.

The old store has just made a wrenching effort at survival and posted a sign on the door saying that it will be open Sundays from one till five, hours that leave its proprietors time for church but not for a proper dinner, not for fishing or softball.

The hardware store will be open on Sunday. This is such a shattering break with tradition, it seems to frighten the customers and they make nervous jokes about it in the aisles, like passengers on a sinking ship.

I carried my chain saw in. The man behind the counter seemed confused, but he took it from me and said, a bit dubiously, "Sure, we can do that for you." He looked around, and then stowed it under the counter. "Have to charge you for it, though."

I said I'd expected to pay.

"No need to bring the whole saw in," he added gently.

Oh. Well, of course I'd known, in theory, that a chain saw blade is detachable, somehow, but mostly this was a source of worry: if it detached itself, like a whirling disembodied set of fangs, what would happen to my arms and legs? It hadn't occurred to me to take the chain off *deliberately*; how would I replace it? and having replaced it myself, would I ever quite trust it again, any more than I trust a tire I have personally fastened to a car?

When I went back to pick it up, the man looked a bit guilty about accepting the modest payment. "Your husband could have done it for you, easy," he said. "Next time, ask your husband."

I didn't tell him that my husband, back when I had one, never went within twenty feet of a chain saw, convinced of its demonic power to spring into life on its own and chase him down the driveway snarling. And I certainly didn't tell him I had no current husband. Around here, not to have a husband is more than just eccentric, it borders on the foolhardy. Women hereabouts marry early and stay married, with good reason.

BACK IN THE FEMINIST SEVENTIES, a T-shirt popular on city sidewalks read, "A woman needs a man like a fish needs a bicycle." Somehow, in the city, it didn't seem like such a silly thing to say. Once you'd acquired one of those toothed squeeze-gadgets for opening the mayonnaise and a landlord who was prompt about sending plumbers, why, except for sentimental reasons, keep a man around?

That was in another world.

Men and women are different. Men are stronger. No matter how many weights I lift, any man still actually warm and breathing will always be stronger than I am. When my car is axle deep in mud or snow, a man can lean his shoulder on the stranded hulk and make it move. Or, if it won't move, he probably knows how to take it apart and reassemble it out on the blacktop.

I buy a sack of sunflower seeds for the bird feeder. I can barely lift it. The helpful clerk carries it out and stows it in my car, taking it for granted that when I get home a man will carry it into the house.

At the county dump, where I'm the only woman wrestling with domestic garbage, I watch the men flip their sixty-pound trash bags over their heads and into the Dumpster as if they were Frisbees.

And I don't care what they tell you, men have a warmer relationship with machinery than women do. Men and machines respect each other. Machines that lark around disobediently for me behave themselves at a single disciplinary glance from a man. Mowers start, logs split, jumper cables attach themselves. Chain saws probably cringe and sharpen themselves.

HUMBLED, I took my saw home, and a few days later, starting off on errands, I rounded a bend to find that a large branch of black locust had blown down across the lane.

The obvious solution was to saw a gap through it. However, my saw, newly sharpened as it was, is electric. A wimpy, girlish saw, totally dependent on household current, tethered like a goat to its home by lengths of orange cord. Gas-powered saws are independent, but they're heavier. I can lift a gas saw up or I can move it sideways, but I can't do both at once, not with any minimal safety.

I didn't need to measure to see that the branch was beyond my saw's range. If I could drive to the hardware store I could buy more lengths of cord, but I couldn't drive anywhere unless I taught my car to jump.

If I were a man I'd have a gas saw, but probably I wouldn't need it now; I'd just move the branch. My imaginary hired man would move the branch. It was wedged on both sides of the lane, meaning I'd need to lift it over my head and wiggle it free before hauling it out of the way. I couldn't lift it higher than my knees.

Once again, I'd have to call for help. I'd have to call C. J. Once again Dudley Doright rescues the shrieking maiden tied to the train tracks. Back to the Stone Age.

C. J. wouldn't mind. Perhaps he even enjoys rescue work. I mind, though. How can I repay him? I came from a world where money paid for everything. It was simple; it was green; it lived in a wallet and was universally accepted. What can I do to pay C. J. that he can't do more easily for himself?

All I can think of is to bake up a batch of cookies and leave them, with a note, in his mailbox.

In the ranks of the militant feminists, consider me stripped of my stripes and drummed clear out of the regiment.

coin of the realm

· · · · · · · · · · · · · · · · ·

Every November, government people are freshly astonished and hurt by their unpopularity. They wonder what they've done wrong and promise to do it differently in the coming year. Actually, at least around here, it can't be anything they've done, because as we see it, they never do anything at all.

At the tavern, someone hoping for a weather forecast has flipped on the local television news. A rush-hour accident on the Washington Beltway is confounding the eastern corridor from Baltimore to Richmond, hardly an uncommon state of affairs. The tavern chortles cynically.

"All they ever do anyway," says Big Mike. "Run out and tie up the morning traffic, then sit around all day so they can go tie up the roads some more."

"It's not like they're doing anything while they're there," says Dave. "Sit at a desk. Makes you wonder why they bother."

"We pay 'em to bother. Pay 'em to go through all that fuss

just so they can sit on their butts and look at the wall. Who's stupid, us or them?"

Washington thinks of itself as a city of workaholics, a city constantly pushed, harried, starved for sleep, rising long before dawn, home long after nightfall. Out here, we see it as unemployed — at our expense. At least if it were sitting on the bench in front of the police station whittling sticks, we wouldn't have to pay it.

We know what "doing" means. Doing is fixing the tractor, nailing shingles on the roof, replacing a rotten fence post, fitting a new handle on the splitting maul, setting up a deer blind, cutting stovewood, hunting around for a used carburetor, and driving off to pick up some pipe joints or to talk to a man about shooting wild turkeys. Nobody ever seems tired, and nobody is ever too rushed to chat with the clerk in the hardware store, but everyone is moving. What could anyone possibly do while sitting at a desk? Play with piles of papers; talk on the phone; look at a computer screen? Idleness, pure and simple. No seated person can pretend to be working. No man who wears a long-sleeved, knee-length outer garment in cold or wet weather can be planning to do any work, not with his arms and legs tied up like that. Work doesn't necessarily imply muscle, but it does imply *motion*.

The women here are in motion, too. When they aren't hoisting their children into supermarket carts and frisking them for packs of stolen gum, they're driving. Miles of blacktop stretch between band practice and soccer and Cub Scouts and the dentist. After their children get cars or pickups of their own, the women drive the same roads to read story hour at the library, run errands at the hospital, teach 4-H clubs to bake and sew, and collect weary housewares for fund-raising rummage sales. Their odometers cycle relentlessly, like clocks.

At night they meet at one another's houses and do crafts. In a more frivolous society they might play cards, but cards here, if not actually satanic, are certainly unproductive — idle. (Bingo, always under the auspices of the local fire and rescue, has the cachet of a good cause.) Their mothers and grandmothers worked with their hands from dawn till bedtime, and what they made was useful; their pieced quilts were for sleeping under, not for framing. They made butter and sweaters, darned socks, sewed buttons, pared apples, held a bottle for an orphan lamb, set out the tomato seedlings, and punched down the bread dough after it doubled in bulk. These women, now their daughters, are proud not to need to do these things; why knit sweaters when there are perfectly good sweaters at the Kmart? Just the same, their hands seem to tingle for employment. Their hands need work the way their lungs need air.

They turn to crafts. They make them on winter evenings while eating home-baked cookies in someone's living room and sell them at our summer fairs and fund-raisers. It seems to be a mark of pride, an essential part of the mystique, that the product be useless. Maybe usefulness would tie them too closely to the drudgery of grandmothers who were forced to make things; circumstance never forced anyone to make a dolly in a calico dress under which to hide the toilet paper, or crochet a star for the Christmas tree, or weave a grapevine wreath, or trim a miniature straw hat with dried flowers and a loop for hanging it on the wall.

The ingredients for these *objets* come from the Ben Franklin store and assembling them is no more challenging than a paint-by-number landscape, but then, making butter wasn't challenging either. These women don't seem to need creative expression, just something to do with their hands. Maybe a leftover current of energy still pulses in the nerves and muscles of their fingers, trapped in our microwavable world.

Probably their daughters won't suffer the same problem. Hands don't matter anymore. My own seem purely vestigial; the only profits they produce, they produce on a keyboard, and even that may be on the way out. I blush to remember what my grandmother could do with hers, and how I can't even pluck a chicken.

IN THIS TRANSITIONAL WORLD, stalled between the orchards and dairy farms and whatever's going to happen next, no one seems to have what city folk would call an *income*, exactly, but no one here mentions money worries — or mentions money at all, for that matter. Few lean on a single career, and this reduces the chance of total disaster. In the winter, the summer farmer plows lanes, cuts and hauls logs, and splits and delivers stovewood. The bartender at the tavern paints houses and restores furniture when he isn't pouring drinks. The clerk in the bike shop trains and sells show horses after hours. A couple of pigs or lambs are no more trouble than one; eat one and sell one.

A bright and feisty woman I know does remember, with a retrospective shudder, the summer she and her husband and their two children lived in their car and ate fish from the river and berries from the roadside until their luck changed, but living off the land here isn't the same as living off the land in Newark or Philadelphia. And luck here, unshackled from résumés and human resources directors, seems more likely to

· · · · · ·

change for the better. You need to give luck some leeway, some room to maneuver.

A person keeps busy, stays in motion, and food and shelter result. Houses are warmed. Freezers are filled with meat and shelves in the cellar are lined with beans and corn in Mason jars. There's even some money. I can't imagine what their tax forms must look like, come April, but then again I can't imagine the IRS auditor valiant enough to tackle that writhing tangle of beeves pastured, fields rented out or mowed, logs trucked, hay and rabbits sold, Christmas geese and turkeys butchered, all the small transactions in constant motion like a coffee can full of healthy fishing worms.

I find that I've slipped into the same way of life, almost without noticing. I clear some brush on the land, freeze tomatoes and raspberries. In trade for hunting rights, people give me venison. I write obituaries and drive around interviewing people on sheep predators, apple trees, and Civil War heroes. I no longer have an income. In the beginning I'd thought I'd be richer here, not paying rent, but then I found out that getting and keeping a country-capable car is the equivalent of a city apartment and hundreds of taxis. Still, I pick up a little something here and there and life, mysteriously, almost miraculously, goes on.

Life without an income is different. At the very least, it's unpatriotic, even subversive, because I'm slow to buy things I don't need and the national economy depends on people buying things they don't need. It also depends on consumer debt and credit, and I go reluctantly into the smallest debt — I made some money this month, but next month, who knows? — and who would give me credit? I've reverted to the days of my youth and save up to buy things, cheating the banks and the credit-card people of their interest money.

Gradually I got over the long habit of wanting things. In the evenings I fill out order forms from catalogs — books, a new sweater, a bigger bird feeder — and in the mornings I reconsider and throw them away. No new sweater is worth the worry of a credit-card balance without a promised income. Besides, I'm not alone. People around me are also wearing their old sweaters and driving their old cars and don't seem the worse for it. In fact, they look quite cheerful. They enjoyed their day.

I enjoy mine, too. Considering the pleasure of waking in the morning to such a mix of things to do — this smorgasbord of work on which to graze — I wonder how I ever sat in an office, the same office, all week. What *was* I doing there from nine till five? Maybe the fellows in the tavern are right: nothing.

AROUND HERE, making money doesn't seem to matter in the urgent way it matters elsewhere, and the rich hereabouts don't get much respect. They're outlanders, for one thing. "Not from around here," as we say. Somehow, except for the man in North Hill who won the lottery, natives never get rich enough to move into the great stone houses with the matching stables. This may be due to the men's widespread contempt for salaried work and their tendency to vanish completely when they think of something better to do.

The rich, who congregate mainly in the southern section of the county famous for Thoroughbreds and polo, came in from away. "Away" tends to mean north of the Potomac River

· · · · · ·

or west of the Ohio, and also applies to the new breed of American nomad, people who have fecklessly lived all over and hence have no true identities at all beyond their poor little meaningless names, names that cast no shadow back into the local past.

"From away" is basically a euphemism for Yankee, which is rarely used and considered rude, as they feel it would be rude to call a colored person "black," a harsh, sharp monosyllable unfriendly in the local mouths. The only time I've heard "Yankee" offered point-blank was in the eye doctor's office, when a patient accused the doctor of being one and added in wondering tones, "I can't understand a word you're saying." "From away" is also used as an excuse for people who behave in public as if they'd had no raising.

Some of the people who now pass as natives were once, like me, from away, but since they came in respectfully and slowly, one family at a time, and accepted the place as they found it, softened their city manners and joined the fire and rescue, nobody holds their origins against them. They're adopted family, but they're family.

The rich don't want to blend in, or perhaps never noticed that there was an in to blend with. Their ignorance, helplessness, and overwrought social lives are a source of entertainment for those who lend them an occasional hand. (The hand is almost always lent outdoors; cooks, chauffeurs, and housekeepers have to be recruited in foreign lands.)

Down at the tavern, Dave reports on his day. "So old Peter comes up in that Land Rover he drives and makes me stop what I'm doing and listen. Says he's going to let me in on a little secret. Key to efficiency, he says. Just remember it and I'll double my work output. Just three little words, he says — he must have read it in a book somewhere — 'Touch nothing twice.' "

General ribaldry, followed by apologies to me, the tavern's token woman.

"So I said," Dave continues, " 'Then I reckon I'll just have to keep all that firewood of yours in my truck, drive it around all winter, since I already touched it loading it up.' Old Peter didn't think that was funny."

If old Peter isn't careful, one of these days Dave will consider himself insulted. He probably won't say anything, but Peter will never see him again.

Perhaps if we had our own hereditary aristocracy here and our grandfathers had worked for their grandfathers, we'd be more respectful, but I doubt it. We aren't respectful by nature. Everyone says "ma'am" — the owner of the general store once called me "ma'am" three times in a single sentence — but nobody says "sir." Dave's forebears didn't come here looking for jobs. They came looking for land, which is quite another matter, and for the few more years that the land's still here, Dave can thumb his nose at Peter and come and go as he pleases. The original rich people, the Carters and Lees and Fairfaxes with land grants of many thousands of acres, were hoping for a European system of serfly tenant farmers; but the immigrants wanted land of their own, and the rich had to fall back on slaves.

This land of small freeholders wasn't designed for hierarchy, except that a man with strong sons and good land had an edge over one with daughters and stony fields. The difference between farmer and farm help was more a matter of mortgage payments than social class. They worked together in the fields, mopping the same sweat, like the farmer's wife and the hired girl canning beans together in August. According to reports, even the farmers' few slaves lived like family; one, the sole woman of the household, was famous as a terrifying tyrant to the widowed farmer and his sons.

In more civilized areas, the social world is a pyramid built of jobs. The chairman of the board sits on top and the walls slope down past the systems analyst and the data-entry clerk to the garbage collector and the chronically unemployed. Out here, the world is flat. The rich aren't on top; they're far off to one side, irrelevant as zebras in a zoo. The rest of us are created pretty equal. Our incomes, when painfully toted up in April, are probably similar, but in any case income doesn't matter much: one job is as good as another. Where there aren't any fancy jobs, there aren't any loathsome ones, either. The county's principal garbage collector calls himself a "garbage-ologist," mocking the pretensions to our east, but he takes his work seriously and patiently collects trash blown everywhere in a storm. We take it seriously too, and consider his labors as useful to the world as any marketing strategist's.

Our underclass, if you could call it that, is prideful and fairly self-sufficient, and charity seems to be more offered than needed. Last year a virtuous group collected mountains of clothing to be given away, no questions asked, to anyone who came. No one came. The organizers, having been to considerable trouble, were quite cross, not to mention having all those clothes to dispose of somehow.

Every year the village at the foot of the mountain takes on a needy family for Christmas, with turkey dinner, a tree, and presents for all. Due to the scarcity of applicants, the same family has received this bounty for three years running and their children now specify acceptable toys by brand name.

BEING CREATED EQUAL sometimes takes me by surprise. In the city, men who came to deliver a couch would deliver, collect their money, and leave, contract fulfilled. They knew I considered them inferior beings, and naturally they hated me. We didn't speak.

Here, it's the custom to offer some light refreshment to workmen after the snow is plowed or the firewood unloaded or the chimney cleaned. They accept it, pull out chairs, and sit down. They take an interest. How old is my cat? How long have I lived here? How do I manage in the winter? Am I ever nervous up here alone at night? Easily, sociably, they offer a bit of mild criticism ("Ought to cut some trees down there, open up the view") and ask if I see many deer, a question usually followed by a request to come hunting in the fall.

What's called "visiting" seems to be a more compelling reason to work than money or status. Women who stayed home alone to raise their children flow joyfully back into the workforce, where they punch the cash registers and weigh the mail smiling, pausing often to visit with neighbors, friends, extended family, and even strangers, inquiring after babies and receiving the gentle scraps of local news. They love their jobs.

Probably the frail old man who sweeps up in the supermarket loves his, too. Certainly he smiles in recognition and offers to help with my groceries as if he was happy to be there, happy to see me. Probably he was bored half silly at home, no longer up to farmwork and sick of watching television.

. . . . . .

Probably *he* thinks swinging a broom out here in the sociable world is a perfectly splendid job.

Back in my city days, the people I knew had their lives and they had their jobs, which they undertook purely in exchange for money, and the two were distinct and incompatible, as if each person spent his days as two people. Around here, jobs and lives seem to be one and the same. Money must matter — surely money always matters? — but it doesn't seem to pay for spending your days doing something you don't want to spend your days doing.

the horns of elfland

· · · · · · · · · · · · · · · ·

Sunday evenings, all summer long, the county gathers on the courthouse lawn to listen to concerts played on the courthouse steps. Carrying babies, baskets, and blankets, they file in through the wrought-iron gate and fan out over the grass, under the last of the big elm trees, miraculously preserved from the blight. They spread out the blankets and lay the babies down to wave their unfocused fists at the leaves overhead. They open their coolers and pass out sodas, potato salad, plates of sliced ham.

I perch on a bench, self-consciously alone. Everyone else, in this world where nobody ever moves away, has brought the family. The whole family. The frail elderly pick their way along the paths with walkers, their elbows held by younger generations. A woman buzzes past me in a motorized wheelchair and toddlers wander from blanket to blanket cadging food. Dogs snooze in the shade.

At a long table covered with a fluttering white cloth the Alzheimer's Respite volunteers are selling fresh lemonade and home-baked cookies. Westering sunlight gilds the bricks of the courthouse.

It's a young courthouse, built in 1894 where the previous courthouses stood, but it has the broad, kindly lines of its predecessors; the white pillars; and the war memorial; and its bell is the original bell of 1769 that rang for the news of the Boston Tea Party, and again when the Declaration of Independence was read aloud, for the first time in Virginia, from the courthouse steps. It still tells the hours.

The concert begins at seven, in sunshine, and goes on through the dusk and into the night. Tonight's band — lead guitar, bass, and drums — plays trucking songs and train songs: "Hot Rod Lincoln," "A Tombstone Every Mile," "Rockabilly Funeral." The summer's music is sometimes classical, sometimes country or jazz or rock: all are welcome.

Singly and in pairs and groups, children leave their families and gather in front of the band to dance barefoot on the warm bricks. Mothers hold the hands of shy little girls and dance with them; fathers dance babies too young to walk. One father cradles a tiny red-haired baby girl and dances her all evening, beaming. Twin girls of about five, immensely self-possessed, dance together until a third child, a little black boy, comes up; they take his hands and the three dance hopping in a ring.

In the shadows behind the courthouse, older children of ten or twelve, scorning to dance, run instead, a long line of them dodging around the big elms. I can see their bare legs flickering through the shadows and doubling back as darkness melts over us.

The lights go on over the bandstand on the steps and still the children dance. Perhaps fifty babies are here and surely over a hundred children, but all evening long not a baby cries, not a child is slapped or scolded, not a voice is raised in anger over the murmurs of laughter and applause.

How can this be happening? Is there a hidden film crew? Surely any minute now a teenage Judy Garland will step shyly into the light, clutch the mike, and sing "Ding, ding, ding went the trolley."

I feel guilty just being here, in this fantasy universe, with my back to reality. I am not in the Black Hills or the Maine woods but only fifty or sixty miles north-northwest of the Washington Beltway. Over there runs the coastal strip that considers itself America. It's a long strip, but from here it feels surprisingly narrow.

The band plays cheerfully on as if for the dedication of the courthouse building a hundred years ago. The dancing children hop and stamp as if somehow the world might pause long enough in its madness for them to grow up and bring their own folding chairs and potato salad to this same peaceable kingdom, and watch their own children twirling barefoot on the bricks as they themselves are doing now.

I ought to stand on the bench, blow a gym whistle, and shout, "*Attention, people! People, please! This is not happening. This is a sentimental dream, foolish nostalgia for a time and place that probably never existed. Go home and read the headlines, go home and turn on the news. Don't you know what time it is? It's now!*"

The lead singer produces a ridiculously huge trombone and blares into "Wabash Cannonball" as, waist-deep in children, he descends the steps. They all fall into line behind him and he leads them, dancing, away into the maze of brick pathways. Laughter floats over the lawn and voices call out:

· · · · · ·

"Take 'em to the river!" "Four blocks down and make a left!" It's full dark now and the line of children vanishes and re-appears as it passes through pools of light and darkness.

I take a firm hold on the back of the bench, as if I too might be tricked into believing this evening and follow the children, seduced by the horns of Elfland into never-never land, somewhere unreachably far beyond the headlines and the evening news.

WHEN WINTER COMES I return to the news on tele-vision, neglected since April. There they still are, Him and Her and Mr. Sports and, if I'm patient enough, eventually Mr. Weather.

I flip back and forth through the three available channels, trying to catch Mr. Weather's fleeting appearance on each. I know he's not going to tell me anything useful, since he works in Washington and wouldn't know real weather if it blew him clear out of the studio, but somehow I feel that it's safer to hear what he has to say. Like looking at the new moon over your left shoulder, it's a magic charm: something possibly dan-gerous to neglect. And maybe, by subtracting ten degrees and adding six inches of snow, I can guess what's going to happen on the mountain.

He's elusive, though. I can't count on him standing by at a given moment on any channel, and when I do find him he's apt to cheat: "How much snow will we get and when will it start? These and other details coming up in our next news hour. Stay tuned." While trying to track his appearances I collect a lot of odd things I wasn't looking for, like lint on a blue suit. I learn things I don't want to know.

I'm not sure just when the news and I began to lose our

grip on each other. I grew up in a news family. There were two newspapers in town then, one that arrived with a thump on the front porch in time to be read at breakfast and a second that came home with the family breadwinner in the evening, to be read after dinner. As we grew, the children of the house progressed slowly from the funnies backward toward the front page. Broadcast news was harvested at least once before bedtime. No event, however meaningless, crept past our house unnoticed.

It was the only responsible, civilized way to live. We were the informed public essential to a democracy, and the state of being informed was a virtuous state. Grown-up, I read the paper every day and watched the news every evening.

Then I moved here to the mountain and the news began to recede. For a long time I pigheadedly went on buying and reading a city newspaper and watching the evening news on television, struggling to keep a grip. It was important to know more than who had died or married within the county. I ought to be able to distinguish among the fragments of the collapsing Russian empire, maybe even to chart the vicissitudes of royal marriages and the prosecution of celebrities.

It was a long trip to buy a newspaper. In good weather I hated to leave the mountain; in bad weather it seemed foolhardy to do so, and in any case the delivery truck probably hadn't made it out as far as North Hill. When I did get a paper, I found myself reverting to childhood, reading it back to front, starting with Ann Landers and the funnies and working my way reluctantly toward the state of the world.

Watching the news on television, I fidgeted and my mind wandered. Perhaps it was no bloodier than it had always been, but I was surrounded by such easygoing people and gentle

· · · · · ·

The Horns of Elfland 63

countryside that bloodshed, except when it involved whitetail deer, began to feel remote and then downright unlikely.

Serbs killed Muslims; Muslims killed Serbs; Israelis and Palestinians killed each other, like Hutus and Tutsis; Haitians and Russians killed other Haitians and Russians, and closer to home, restless folk killed strangers to express their political views or simply to try out a new gun. I sat and watched, and outside my dark windows foxes were afoot and owls were afloat, looking for my round-eared, bright-eyed field mice to kill, but they were hungry. As far as I could tell from the news, none of these people were eating their victims. If they were, it would make better sense, but they seemed to be always on the move, tearing around with tanks and field artillery, scarcely a moment to sit down to a meal.

Even our deer hunters here, so horrifying to civilized folk, bind themselves to the rule that you eat what you kill. Perhaps the United Nations should consider adding that rule to warfare; at least pausing to cook and dine would slow the pace of chaos.

What clinched it was the kid and the swimming pool. In the summer, in a city neighborhood, a kid with an assault gun was passing a community swimming pool full of other kids and opened fire. Some were killed and some were wounded. The reporter reported from in front of the pool, now mercifully drained. He said there was no apparent motive. It was just one of those things.

Abruptly, from several feet beyond my left ear, a voice spoke to me. I didn't recognize the voice, but it had an authoritative, auntlike ring to it. "They're making it up, you know," she said. "They make it all up." And the invisible aunt-figure reached across my lap to the remote control.

. . . . . .

I still buy a Sunday paper and read most of it, though some Sundays I never quite make it clear through to the front. It may be a tissue of lies. Even the newspapers might be making it up. They, too, have a living to earn.

SOMETIMES PEOPLE CALL ME from out there in the important world. In the fall — I'm not sure just when, but the first maples were starting to turn on the mountain — an editor called, and apologized for calling. "Were you watching television? I wanted to be sure to call you before verdict time."

"Before verdict time," I repeated carefully.

"At one," she said. "It's at one."

I pulled myself together. "You mean in the Simpson trial? But I thought the jury just went out. Or didn't they?" I stalled, shamed.

The editor was enchanted with my innocence. "I can't believe I've had the chance to actually tell someone who didn't know. Don't you watch television? Or listen to the radio? You don't hear the news?"

"I work for the county newspaper," I said, gathering up my dignity. "I know all the news. We're busy, we've got an important election coming up," I added defensively.

"Election? That's a whole year away," she said.

"It's next month," I said firmly. "But thank you for telling me about the Simpson trial."

At the appointed hour I turned on the radio. Simpson was acquitted. I turned it off again. The next day, on my errands, I dutifully picked up a newspaper. A city newspaper, not our county weekly, which wouldn't mention it. The whole front page was about O. J. Simpson's acquittal. The country, it said, had come to a complete standstill over the matter.

· · · · · ·

The Horns of Elfland 65

I dropped the paper on the table and combed my hair for candidates' night in the village.

The meeting, like all our meetings, was held in the community center that used to be our village school before the Pied Piper went through centralizing the schools. The auditorium was packed and long tables at the back sagged under the home-baked cakes and cookies so essential to politics. Every candidate for every office was there, accompanied by friends and family and flack, easily outnumbering the villagers. Two babies were in attendance; they took turns crying. Many small children in their hard-soled school shoes ran noisily around on a floor freshly varnished for morning aerobics classes.

Each candidate had five minutes to speak, and when the time was up a villager in the front row held out a big kitchen clock and pointed to it. I'd forgotten to bring anything to write on and struggled to remember all the names and whether I liked them or not. That oily fellow running for commonwealth's attorney, now, his name began with an A. A *for ass*, I told myself. I must remember. The long-incumbent sheriff still looked good, his silver star twinkling on his breast; his opponent was ex-CIA and seemed to think sophisticated high-tech experience mattered for local sheriffry, here where our major crime is drunk driving. And who were those people running for county treasurer? And how strange to have to vote for one for the first time; the previous man had always run unopposed and was now retiring after thirty-seven years. We'll have to throw away mountains of tax bills and envelopes traditionally printed with his name.

The chairs at the community center are agony, and from time to time small groups stepped outside to stretch and

. . . . . .

smoke in the mild foggy night. We talked about the election and about the new lights out front — tall, powerful pole lights that weren't turned on for the occasion. The county bought them and came and installed them, but we don't like them. They keep the dark village awake. The civilized goal of lighting the outdoors in the hours of God's darkness is still alien here.

Candidates rose and spoke and sat again, and my head ached with them. All I could remember was A for ass. All called themselves either Democrats or Republicans, but that doesn't make a shred of difference here, where all our issues are local ones. A good thing, too, since in larger ideological matters I stand, to judge from the bumper stickers, fields apart from the local majority. With their natural good manners, folk seem to sense this and refrain from bringing them up, and I have finally grown old enough to keep my mouth shut.

Our burning local issues are all the same issue — land use: the loss of farms; the arrival of shopping centers; rezoning and development and their attendant schools and roads and taxes. Housing developments are raising our school population by 10 percent every year. Taxes go up with each new school we build, forcing more farmers to close down and sell their land to developers, who build more houses that need more schools.

Voting doesn't have the slightest effect on these matters, but somehow we keep voting anyway. We care. Everywhere I drive, front lawns are brightly bannered with the names of candidates. Sometimes next-door neighbors, disagreeing, have each put up dozens of opposing signs, all in primary colors like the flags of the United Nations. Tirelessly the candidates show up to speak at every community center, every picnic, every school, except in the one small town where there are

· · · · · ·

no candidates. By tradition there, nobody files to run for office. The citizens write in the names, and those who get the most votes have to serve whether they want to or not.

In this village of Pikestown, sixty miles from the White House, the whole Washington tribe looks wispy and insubstantial. They've come to seem purely theoretical, a mere formality. It matters who wins the race for district supervisor and how he or she feels about sewers; who gets to be president simply may not matter much. Things over there seem to muddle along one way or the other, and a country that survived Franklin Pierce and Warren G. Harding is probably pretty tough.

Our village, on the other hand, is fragile. Our village, as a village, could be wiped out overnight by a couple of signatures, the way North Hill will be soon, its population poised to leap from a friendly five hundred to a shapeless, unfocused five thousand.

It was late when the meeting finally wore itself out and I found my car and drove home. On the mountain the fog was so thick I had to open the door and look down to steer along the yellow line. Elections always take place in fog season, I mused, which may or may not be significant. A for ass. Only I'd forgotten what he was running for. And one of the school-board candidates was obviously a splendid fellow while the other seemed a touch hysterical, but which was which? My pockets were stuffed with flyers to study at leisure.

At home, the city paper still lay reproachfully on the table. I thumbed through it. Every section except the classified ads was solid O. J. Simpson. The entire nation, possibly the entire world, had talked about nothing else for days now.

I had spent the evening surrounded by people, by neigh-

· · · · · ·

bors and earnest office seekers, and chatted with a dozen of them, and the name of the man of the hour never crossed our lips.

I was embarrassed. Were we so provincial, then, so self-centered, so insular, so far out of the loop that we thought of nothing but ourselves and our petty concerns, our roads and zoning laws, while major news rocked the world? How could we ignore the riveting event of the decade? How could I ever visit a city again and talk to civilized folk, all countrified as I was?

Or, on the other hand, perhaps only we out of the whole nation had spent the evening — had spent the previous months of the trial, for that matter — keeping our eye on the ball: minding our own shop. Managing our own lives and trying to keep a grip on our own small world, however insignificant in the global scheme.

Hopelessly provincial? Or just sensible? I couldn't decide, though I did remember the name of the woman I liked for district supervisor. The newspaper somehow resisted being read, but I couldn't very well just ignore it.

I folded it up and shoved it into a bookshelf. I really would have to read all about it. One of these days.

the orderly life

· · · · · · · · · · · · · · · · ·

It's considered almost as unseemly for a woman to live alone on the mountain all year round as it is for her to sit on a barstool, but for her to live alone without a dog is simply preposterous. Workmen and deliverymen remind me, when they call for directions, to tie up my dogs before they arrive. When they do arrive and find no visible dog, they're shocked.

I have cats, I offer, and they look perplexed: What do cats have to do with it? Cats are for the barn, to keep down mice. Dogs are for the house, to keep down burglars.

Everyone here has dogs, usually a pair of them, usually large. During small-game season those of suitable breed are allowed to go hunting, but the rest of the year they're attached to the house, sometimes by a chain. Their owners proudly announce that they've never been robbed, never even glimpsed a robber. As they see it, this isn't because there aren't any robbers, but because the robbers, hearing or seeing dogs, slink back away down the lane like the cowardly, lily-livered scum that they are.

Dogs are the crime deterrent of choice. Naturally every household is heavily armed as well, here in hard-core hunting country, but these people know guns too well to rely on them for nailing moving targets in the country dark. A pair of Labs will do the job, warding off burglars the way garlic wards off witches or a piece of iron in the pocket protects against magic spells.

The existence of burglars, like the existence of magic spells, must be taken on faith.

In the eastern, civilized part of the county we get the usual civilized break-ins and holdups and drug busts, but out here in the wilderness we make for dull reading. The cops-and-courts reporter at the paper is often found covering high-school graduations and library-board meetings for lack of proper employment.

Aside from driving under the influence, our most prevalent crime is the stealing of toolboxes from the unsheltered beds of pickup trucks. Not much else gets stolen, and when the mailman has a package too big for my mailbox he simply props it against the post, up there at the side of the county road, where it stays until I collect it. When I find my wallet missing I simply check back over my itinerary: Will it be waiting for me in the library, the drugstore, by the bank machine? On the dashboard of my unlocked car? But our criminals — and our honest men, too — are mesmerized by tools. They covet them the way city men covet wealth and distinction; perhaps here tools *are* wealth and distinction. Men use them, collect them, lend them, oil and arrange and sharpen them, and occasionally, overcome with lust, steal them. The rightful owner, who had merely stopped off for a beer or to buy another tool in the hardware store, howls as if his children had been kidnapped.

One solution might be to lock the toolbox in the cab of the truck, but apparently this isn't satisfactory. There's an unspoken feeling here that locking a door, any door, is an unneighborly act. Mean-spirited. So the prudent simply add one of the watchdogs to the truck bed, beside the toolbox. This works pretty well, since the would-be criminal respects the idea, the concept, of a watchdog, however cheerfully it smiles and waves its tail at passersby.

Other crime tends to be sui generis. Recently the entire transmission was stolen from an elderly Ford pickup truck asleep in its own driveway, under the nose of watchdogs. Last summer a tractor, complete with mower blade, was stolen overnight from a field, which seems like conspicuous loot. Did no late traveler wonder, swooping around the tractor on the highway as the miscreant made his getaway at eight miles an hour, what agricultural business it was pursuing after midnight? Apparently not.

Both criminals are still at large.

Last year a zealous new cops-and-courts reporter, desperate for action, persuaded the editor to let him run the pictures and crimes of the county's ten most-wanted men on page A1. The mug shots were a bit smudged, but apparently eight were white, one Hispanic, one black, and all deeply embarrassed. Their crimes ranged from bad checks to failure to report to a parole officer.

The following morning, at the front desk, a pleasant-spoken

young man came in and surrendered to our two pretty receptionists. "I didn't realize," he said. "I didn't know they were looking for me, I didn't know anything about it till a friend of mine saw the paper and called me."

Doris and Donna explained that, as a newspaper, we weren't equipped to arrest people, and pointed out the courthouse across the street. He thanked them, and was seen through the window going in through the iron gates and up the brick path to justice.

Last summer the sidewalk bench was stolen from in front of the candy store. The candy store set out a chalkboard easel in its place, asking that the bench be returned to its home. A week later, sometime in the night, it was. The chalkboard was set beside it, welcoming it back from its travels in parts unknown and thanking its "traveling companions" for its safe return.

And only the other day, a customer in Payne's Biker Bar, across the street from the courthouse, spotted a couple of sheriff's deputies on its lawn and rushed out to the sidewalk among the Harleys and mooned them. He was arrested and charged with indecent exposure and released on his own recognizance.

And fifty years ago or thereabouts, crime struck on the mountain itself: A man on the other side of the Gap shot and killed his brother-in-law in a dispute about a pig. As the story is told, the pig produced piglets while on loan to the first man, who then returned her, but felt he had a right to keep the offspring.

No one explains why anyone would want to borrow a pig in the first place. Unlike cows and hens, pigs come into their financial glory only after death. Perhaps the party of the first part was simply pig-sitting while his brother-in-law was away? It's too late to know.

Anyway, anxious to conform to local custom, sometimes I think about getting a dog, but I have nothing rural worth stealing. Such tools as I own are contemptibly feminine. The city criminal coming for my antique computer would have a long drive from the better-lit places where burglars live; the darkness here would be daunting. My lane is four-wheel-drive country, dangerously steep, pocked with holes, and alternately icy and muddy. In the headlights, brambles reach out across the ruts like witches' claws. The car strains and wallows, the gravel crunches, fallen branches crack. A car's approach by night wakes me from a hundred yards away.

Frightening them, warning me: What dog could do more? My road is my watchdog. It doesn't run to greet me at the door, but then it doesn't need feeding and never gets fleas. And so far it hasn't been called upon to bark.

Cleaning out the kitchen cupboard, I came across a can of Mace left over from my city days and gazed on it with wondering eyes: Did I really set forth at night to visit friends with Mace in one pocket and a twenty-dollar bribe in the other? Did I really call my host and hostess to report my safe arrival home? Check the window locks before I went to bed? What a waste of energy and spirit; what an awkward way to live, surrounded by people who wished to do me harm.

I was used to it, of course. Most people are. Most people barely notice now how much time and spirit they spend fussing over their safety and the security of their chattels, or how uncomfortable the matter is in their minds, all sharp corners and dark shadows. It can't be good for us. It must do damage, knowing all day long and into the night's sleep that the world is a hostile place. Probably it breeds reciprocal hostility, until even the meekest citizen knows the urge to harm something, someone — anyone — in return.

It took me months here to adjust. In official places I felt naked and exposed when speaking face-to-face with people who should have been behind bulletproof glass, as if one or both of us had already been convicted of a felony. The postmistress and I leaned our elbows on the counter and looked each other in the eye when passing the time of day. It seemed almost obscenely intimate that money was passed directly from hand to hand instead of poked through slots and that every place of business accepts personal checks with no questions asked.

Except in the new chain stores where they're mandated from headquarters, there are no surveillance cameras. Shopping, I felt strangely adrift not to be shadowed by security guards; nobody here thinks I want to steal their merchandise. In the city, the hot glare of suspicion seemed like a challenge, and I often thought it would be sporting to outwit the guards and checkpoints and cameras and pocket a lipstick or a roll of film. Theft would be a personal triumph, something to brag about. Here, they trust me, and I'd sooner starve than steal an apple.

I left my scarf in the dentist's office and didn't miss it. At dinnertime the phone call came; the dentist's receptionist had called her way down the full day's list of clients and I was the last, so the scarf, she figured, had to be mine.

IN THE CITY, the word "trust" referred to banking institutions. Here, it came to mean I could walk around knowing

· · · · · ·

that my fellow citizens would make a real effort not to harm me, even by accident, even at busy intersections. Very slowly I got used to living among people of goodwill and grew nicer myself. Remembered to say please and thank you to waitress and gas-station attendant. Smiled more. A whole section of alertness in my head went slack, sagged, and let go, until even in deepest sleep I knew that a crash in the living room meant the cat had knocked the phone off the table again and rustling noises outside meant that creatures were hunting for their breakfast, not for me.

I don't know anything about the functions of the human mind, but I tend to think of it as physical and limited, like a closet: if it's stuffed with one thing, there won't be room for more. And I can put my hand on my head now and almost feel the extra space inside, freshly vacated by my wariness and street smarts. Perhaps I'll try to learn how the computer works. Maybe dig into Chinese history or the medieval church, polish up my rusty French. There's room for it now, and the empty space feels brighter, as if what I used to know about the world had been a dark and possibly toxic burden all day long.

DOWN IN THE VALLEY, as everywhere, the crime rate among the young soars in the summer months, but here in the rural western county, according to the newspaper, all their crimes are the same crime: field parties. Fifty or a hundred of our high-school students will gather in a hay field, by invitation of the son or daughter of the farm, and drink beer and play music. As one young host told a reporter, "I figured if someone threw up in the field, it wouldn't matter like in the house."

. . . . . .

The police admit they have trouble making arrests. A field is not a living room, and its surrounding woods provide generous cover for this as for other wildlife. A spokesman from the sheriff's office said, "Five hundred kids will run in five hundred different directions. I'm lucky if I write up ten."

The level of public outrage remains low. Nobody here is yet conditioned to think of loose teenagers as a menace; nobody sees their summer freedom as a ticking bomb. For reasons that might bear investigating, our kids are good kids.

They seem to enjoy a higher social status here than in city or suburb; perhaps this is a relic of the farming world in which children are useful and valuable instead of expensive decorations. They're respected coworkers responsible for work more substantive than cleaning up their rooms; they're trusted with expensive livestock and machinery.

The new people moving into the new developments are bringing children from a different tradition, and the sheriff's department, used to its own, is dumbfounded by what's only perfectly normal teenage crime — shoplifting, vandalism, graffiti, an occasional borrowed car. In just the past twelve months, juvenile drug arrests tripled. The deputies understand drugs and theft, but vandalism seems to mystify them: Why would anyone want to damage things? Pull up the new shrubbery around the new post office and break windows in their own new school? Our police don't seem to realize that it's the new kids who are normal and our own who are out of step with the world.

Recently we were all scandalized by the beating to death, by kids with baseball bats, of a goose who wouldn't abandon her nest to escape her tormentors. To us it seemed sickening

· · · · · ·

almost beyond belief, but the kids themselves were mystified by our fuss.

An Englishwoman who works for the paper was unsurprised. She said it was just like World War II, when English children from endangered areas were evacuated to the welcoming countryside. The country folk couldn't understand the pleasure the children took in breaking things and hurting animals. The children, in turn, couldn't understand why anyone minded; where they came from, pastimes like stoning swans to death and using hedgehogs for footballs, while hardly sanctioned, were basic to the childhoods of the middle class.

"They weren't evil children," she said. "They simply came from a different culture. Most of them grew up just fine, I'm sure."

The children of the natives here still maintain a curiously high level of general virtue. They don't crowd pedestrians off the sidewalk, they hold doors open for me, their cars and pickups pass by laying only the gentlest of country music onto the air. They never seem angry.

Of course, their parents and neighbors aren't angry, either, and here in the land of toilets still labeled Ladies and Gentlemen, they don't misbehave in public. Anyone complaining to a waitress or quarreling audibly must not be, as we say, from around here.

Like their elders, the young go to church. They've been going to church since their crayoning days in the infants' Bible class. They take church-sponsored trips and volunteer for church-sponsored projects and turn out with their families for church picnics.

Several years ago a high-school class stirred up a hornets' nest by voting almost unanimously to pray at their graduation ceremonies. In the eastern, suburbanized part of the county, protests were raised and the guardians of our civil liberties marched thundering into the fray. Lawsuits were threatened, injunctions were granted and then suspended, and ultimately a student did close the ceremonies with a brief prayer of her own devising. At its end, one graduate produced a loud, faked sneeze, followed by a general chorus of "God bless you," sealing the victory of communal faith over individual liberty.

It was a short victory, though. The civil-libertarian voices in the east were only biding their time, and a year and a half later, Christmas was swept from the schools in a single stroke, leaving not a telltale whiff of frankincense behind. Christmas in the school system was replaced by winter: winter concerts, winter pageants, winter holidays, though somehow slush and ice seem less cheerful cause for rejoicing. Items in the canon irreversibly stained with Christmas, like *The Nutcracker*, limped on disguised as "traditional," folkloric rather than Christian, but their days, too, may be numbered. Just across the mountains to the west, Christianity remains as two-fisted and unanimous as ever, but here, the tide of multiculturalism is nibbling at our shores.

WHEN SCHOOL CLOSES IN JUNE, the young fan out into the labor market. Some of the boys work with their fathers, pursuing their true education in how to drive a nail straight or fix whatever ails the tractor. Others make change, pump gas, pick peaches, bag groceries, finish their 4-H projects, and volunteer at the hospital or the libraries. If disaster has struck somewhere in the world, they're out washing cars to raise funds and collecting canned goods to send. Their amiable faces are everywhere, all summer.

. . . . . .

The Orderly Life 79

An ex-mother, I watch them closely. In the supermarket, the girl ringing up my groceries is conspiring with another girl in undertones. "You could come over to my house and do it," she says, her hands stalled among my cat-food cans. "While my mother's not home. Who's going to know? And after all, there's nothing your mother can do to you after it's already done."

What dark deeds are these? I draw myself up and say firmly, "Speaking as a mother, let me tell you there's *plenty* she can do to you."

They turned their earnest faces to me. "Well, gee," said the second girl. "For dyeing my hair...?"

Dark deeds indeed. "Don't call it dyeing," I advise. "Say 'coloring,' it sounds better."

"How about 'enhancing'?"

"Better still. Sounds almost educational, doesn't it?"

The conspirators giggled.

Opportunities for the restless to run off their insurgency are scarce around here. In fact, they're limited to driving over to the next county to the west, where the train tracks still cross Main Street, and dodging around the crossing gates to the warning dings and the chuff of the approaching train.

Otherwise, they behave themselves. I despaired of them, so sincere, so pious, so anxious to be good. So respectable, with their neat clothes and clean hair and beardless chins. What would I have thought of them when I was their age? I would have scorned them as spiritless, unimaginative syco-phants and sheep. I would have said that anyone without the creative urge to spray-paint his name on a bridge at sixteen wasn't likely to leave his mark on the world later.

Then I read about their field parties and rejoiced. Like

werewolves, after their virtuous day with the cash register or the tractor, they convene in the pasture to bay the moon. I envied them their midnight Woodstocks among the grazing steers, under the clean sky, where everyone has always known everyone else and the substance of choice is beer.

Later some may drive home with a skinful, but some will have sober, preappointed drivers, and others will fall asleep in the field, to wake up aching and squinting in the blazing sun and take up the virtuous life again.

I know it's wicked to encourage crime in the young — and drinking beer under the age of twenty-one is a crime, if not a sin — but I can't help being glad that these good children will have something merrier to look back on at forty than Sunday-school picnics and high-school basketball. God knows they deserve it.

WHEN THE SCHOOLS REOPEN in September, the pace of life in the valley, though never brisk, picks up a bit. Schools are central to life here. In cities, school superintendents complain that parents take no interest, no part in the scholastic world. Here parents, collateral relatives, and even neighbors seem to spend as much time hanging around schools as the kids do. They volunteer in the lunchroom, coach sports, raise money, and give inspirational talks on team spirit. Schools are a family matter. In the fall, the elementary schools all hold a Grandparents Day, with every confidence that each child will have two full sets on hand.

In the high schools a small cadre of students, duly honored at a banquet in the spring, goes in for abstract matters like Advanced French, but sports are the real core curriculum. We pay respectful lip service to book learning, especially in the lower grades, and we do realize the children should learn to read and write, divide and multiply, and use a computer, but by high school, team sports are the heart and soul of education.

Everyone takes part. Taking part is a moral imperative, a required course, the measure of one's worth. Children who simply cannot learn to catch or throw a ball of any shape join the marching band that plays at halftime, so as not to be shut out utterly from the world of school; their parents raise funds for uniforms and instruments and trips. Even the remotest relatives go to the games and restrain themselves from diving onto the field to stop a grounder. We have four high schools in the county, playing each other tirelessly around the school year, and the newspaper covers every game.

In summer, with the schools closed, the paper shrinks and the sports editor idles around in the lunchroom. The photographers find their weekends suddenly free. A hollow spot opens in the heart of the county. Oh, we still have our other social mainstays, church and the volunteer fire and rescue squads, and these try to take up the slack with sponsored bus trips to discount malls or theme parks, bingo, fund-raising rummage sales, and minifairs in the Kmart parking lot. Life's not the same, though. It lacks dynamic tension. There's a sense of isolation, as if, in July and August, neighbors were separated from one another by snowdrifts. School brings them together again.

As soon as the doors reopen, the parents of high-school seniors cluster in groups to plan for June. Every year they throw what's called, with each word capitalized, the All-Night Drug- And Alcohol-Free After-Graduation Party. They decide on a theme, such as Caribbean Cruise or Mardi Gras. (No one is so wicked or so worldly as to wonder what an alcohol-free Mardi Gras could possibly look like.) Through the winter they meet regularly, and spring peaks in a frenzy of activity, of decorations, costumes, menus, games, contests, musical groups, and displays of the graduates' baby pictures. When the actual party rolls around, culmination of nine months' preparation, parents eagerly volunteer to chaperone it, reliving their own youth, quite possibly at their old school.

The next day must be a letdown. If the graduate was their youngest, they face a slack future of bus trips and bingo, at least until the grandchildren come. Still, they're as proud of their graduates as if they'd invented the wheel; they congratulate them publicly. The newspaper admires them in print and publishes their pictures.

Far away in the sophisticated suburbs, high school is a stepping-stone, a bridge, and its purpose is to groom the young for college and four more years of youth. Here, it's less a bridge than a destination. Graduates become adults. Some go on to take courses in computers, accounting, or nursing, but those are held in places that have no team sports and so can't be considered *school*. A few, proudly reported in the paper, do go away to colleges, though rarely more than two hours' drive from their beloved turf. High school and its playing fields hold firm in the heart.

There on the basketball court or the softball diamond our citizens were bonded forever to their future neighbors, to the cop who will pull them over for speeding, the clerk in the supermarket, the building contractor who will sign their paycheck, the parents of their child's best friend.

In the paper's wedding announcements, the bride and groom have often graduated from the same high school in

......

successive years. In later life, even in their obituaries, it will be recorded whether they went to County or to Valley; friends will remember the no-hitter she pitched there.

Where kids routinely go away to college, often never to wholly return, high school is a preparation for leaving and graduation tastes bittersweet, a bon voyage party, all flowers and tears. Friends vow to stay in touch, but secretly they know this means good-bye. Parents know it too.

Here, high school is a preparation for staying. This has very little to do with Advanced French and everything to do with the lifelong company of former teammates and the nourishment of loved, familiar places.

native soil

• • • • • • • • • • • • • • • •

If, like me, you grew up and went to school among northerners, you think — when you think of it at all — that the Civil War was all about slavery and happened a long time ago. Then if, like me, you move to Virginia, you learn that it was all about Northern aggression and happened day before yesterday.

People here are just as ignorant of history in general as the rest of the country is said to be. Not scholarly by nature, they see no practical need to clutter their heads with tariff legislation and who shot President McKinley. The War Between the States, though, is something else. People here know it easily, warmly, lovingly, the way they know the family legends of crazy Aunt Dora, or the road across the river to Winchester where once we ambushed Sheridan's wagon train.

Even strangers can tell the players apart because we speak of our own by their full and proper names — "Robert E. Lee," "Nathan Bedford Forrest" — while the opposing team is last-name-only: "McClellan," "Grant." We know them all.

They're our tribal totems. The housewife knows them. The mailman knows them.

It happened here. Down in the Deep South, the menfolk went away and many of them died; everyone suffered later under Reconstruction. But for actual fighting and damage, the difference between the war in our valley and the war in Alabama was like the difference between spending World War II in London or in Montana. Our fat valley farmlands were a good place to feed an army, either army, and collect some fresh horses. Only a shallow river separated us from the North, and any man, woman, or child can show you the spot where we pushed the Yankees back over the bluff and into the water. (Young Oliver Wendell Holmes was wounded in the chest there, but seems to have survived.) The Blue Ridge runs down the land as a barricade to the West, and both armies surged and struggled through its three narrow gaps. My own Gap is so slender that any kid with a squirrel-hunting gun could pick off anyone headed to Winchester or back. Where I turn onto the mountain road from the highway, our boys set up cannons loaded with canister and chased the Eighth New York back down the hill. When the valley was occupied by Feds, Mosby and his Rangers, who used it as a base, could scatter up the mountain by deer trails as far as my front yard and keep a watch over happenings below.

We had the whole war. As one of our many local historians likes to say, "People in Gettysburg had a bad week; people here had a bad four years." We don't much bother with far-away events like Vicksburg, but we know what happened here. We know the names of the colonels and we can drive you to the very spot.

. . . . . .

Battle reenactments are our Saturday-afternoon outings; we pack a picnic lunch and bring the kids. For evening meetings on boring subjects, citizens are enticed into coming by the promise of a Civil War lecturer, and they turn off the television, bundle up, and attend. Hard to imagine ordinary folk north of the Mason-Dixon Line being drawn by such a lure. And how many northerners remember their own Reynolds, Doubleday, Sickles, and Buford and what they did at Gettysburg? Even in Gettysburg, how many remember? But this is Virginia, called "the mystic dirt of love."

Rototillers turn up bullets and buttons. A house down the road preserves a hole in the door made by a Yankee artillery shell; the shell itself serves as a doorstop. It's easy to remember a war when you keep stubbing your toe on a shell that slammed into your dining room.

You don't need to inherit the War. You can move into it in a rental truck, all unsuspecting, the way I did, and find yourself absorbing the folklore out of the air. I know that six of the ten original companies in the Bloody Eighth Virginia were made up of local county boys, but I don't know why I know it. I cross the river into Maryland on a ferryboat called the *Jubal Early*; I know who he was, and I know his middle name. It came to me out of thin air.

It's hard not to learn. For the time being, it's all still here. The roads and mountain gaps are the same roads and gaps. Here are the stone walls they crouched behind; there's the sloping field they charged up under fire. The villages have shrunk a bit and some of the roads have been paved, but you can still go to Sunday service in the church where they nursed the wounded. You can trace their initials scratched in the wall. This past summer a hardy band of reenactors camped out there overnight and several of them saw an indisputable, glowing ghost; the whole platoon left the premises.

You can still see the shape of the land. You can still say, the Fourth Virginia was in this field, the Seventh Indiana came up this lane.

Nobody here cares about history, and Jefferson may be the only president they can think of offhand, but the War—ah, the War! That's our here-and-now, our nursery rhyme, barroom gossip, family album, bedtime story, playground game. Our roads and creeks and fields.

Visiting northerners, who have never fought and lost a war in their own streets and fields, are shocked by this pervasive knowledge. They think we must regret the good old days of slavery and mint juleps, and pine in our hearts to set our black neighbors to toiling in the cotton fields again, but we never had any cotton fields, and I haven't seen a mint julep since I left Philadelphia; iced tea is the national drink of Virginia, served by the pailful on all occasions. And our black neighbors, mostly small farmers and independent contractors like the rest of us, generally live in their own houses: some in the small old towns like Brownsville and St. Louis, founded by free blacks before the War; some simply mixed in with the rest of us, after the southern custom. Some of their ancestors were slaves; some owned slaves themselves.

In supermarket and parking lot, blacks and whites touch each other freely, slap each other's shoulders over a joke. Out back at the newspaper where I'm loitering, a young black man from the pressroom sits tilted back in a lawn chair in the sun. A plump blond woman comes out and says, "Hey there, man, you getting a suntan?" Without opening his eyes he says, "I don't want no suntan, I'm black enough." Both chortle, and she slaps him happily several times across the thighs before passing on still chuckling.

When my mother was building this house, she was given the name of the best stonemason in the area. He was the great-grandson of a slave who'd been famous for his stonework and proudly rented out by his owner to build for selected neighbors. When the great-grandson came to build mother's chimney and fireplaces, he brought his son as an assistant and a grandson no more than eight or nine as an apprentice, allowed to fetch and carry and watch.

Halfway through the job, they picked up their tools and left. President and Mrs. Kennedy were working on a house down in the southern part of the county where the rich people live, and they, too, had been given the name of the best stonemason in the area. Mother bowed to superior authority; the chimney waited patiently until the family returned, reputation freshly burnished.

Now in the evenings I consider my fireplace, each stone left rough and natural but perfectly fitted, the various colors blending seamlessly, and think that not even presidents, not even *rich* presidents, have a finer chimney.

The War Between the States is the common mythology that binds us together, but this isn't magnolia-blossom South and there's no nostalgia in the tales. This is the finest, deepest, richest soil in the east, and we always grew food crops here, never cotton or tobacco. A man, white or black, with a hardworking wife and sturdy sons hardly needed the expense and trouble of slaves to make a living. And slavery, the central issue of the War in northern eyes, seems to have left no echoes in our stories. The Confederate battle flag, perennial bone of contention in the Deep South, appears here only at reenactments.

Neither is there the rancor my northern friends look for. The storytellers even shrug philosophically over Sheridan ordering Merritt to burn our valley. Militarily speaking, it was the only thing to do.

Merritt's men burned the crops. They burned the barns with the winter's hay and grain. They captured or drove off the horses — though one family saved its riding horse, Old Fox, by hiding her in the parlor. (We even remember the *horses'* names.) They shot and burned the cows and pigs and chickens. They smashed open the smokehouses and threw the winter's hams on the fire while mothers wept on their knees.

I look down from my deck at the valley that burned and stank and smoldered for five days. Sometimes I can almost smell the smoke. It smells of meat and feathers.

Reasonable, though, the storytellers say. We were feeding and sheltering Mosby's Rangers and his raids were a plague to the Yankees. They were trying to starve the Rangers out. It didn't work.

Down at the newspaper, a new reporter, come from away, wrote a story about a Civil War battlefield. The editor considered it, rocked back and forth from heel to toe, and said, "There's just one thing wrong with it. You didn't mention Mosby."

"Mosby? There wasn't anyone named Mosby there."

"Of course not. He didn't do *battles.* Just drag his name in somehow. At this newspaper we've got one hard-and-fast rule on Civil War stories — "

In ragged chorus the newsroom chanted, *"Mention Mosby."*

. . . . . .

Every proper mythology needs a senior god. Down to our southwest, every dish on the menu is named for Stonewall Jackson; here, Mosby — *Colonel John Singleton* Mosby — rules. He did adventures rather than battles, and he didn't follow orders. Nobody could find him to give him orders. He was an independent contractor, like so many of us here. He knew the country, and he looked around and did whatever seemed best to him at the time, like so many of us here.

We tell each other Mosby stories:

GENERAL STOUGHTON WAS ASLEEP, as well he might be. He was safely at Fairfax Court House, twenty miles inside his own lines in northern Virginia, and snuggled among three regiments of his cavalry, two of infantry, and a smattering of artillery. Besides, there were several empty champagne bottles on his bedside table. He slept soundly.

When a rude stranger burst into his bedroom and yanked off his quilts, he only curled up like a fetus. The stranger snatched up his nightshirt and gave the exposed Yankee rump a violent spank, and the general woke up sputtering. He said, "Do you know who I am? I will have you arrested, sir!"

"Do you know who *I* am?" asked the stranger. "Have you ever heard of Mosby?"

"Yes!" cried the general. "Have you caught the damned rascal?"

"No, but he has caught you."

At least, that's the way Mosby told it. Other accounts vary a bit, but it was indisputably a coup, and John Singleton Mosby and his cohorts took the befuddled general back to Rebel territory, along with two Union captains, thirty Union

· · · · · ·

enlisted men, fifty-eight excellent Union horses, and selected portable goods.

Cub Run was in flood and everyone had to swim, including Stoughton, who must have been quite sober by then. Dripping, he said, "Captain, this is the first bad treatment I have received at your hands."

The next day Mosby delivered his prize to General Fitzhugh Lee at Culpeper. Lee and Stoughton had been classmates at West Point and promptly disappeared into the nice warm headquarters together to chat about old times, while Mosby waited outside in the rain.

Unlike most of the officers on both sides, he'd never been to West Point. He wasn't one of the Old Boys. In fact, he'd been a small-town lawyer before the Civil War offered him more amusing options.

History buffs sometimes marvel that this respectable little man with a wife and two children suddenly changed, like Superman in a phone booth, into the most colorful of Confederate heroes, but Mosby had never been Clark Kent. While at the University of Virginia, where he excelled in Latin, Greek, and literature, he was fined ten dollars for breaking a gunstock over a constable's head. In his final year he shot a town bully who had insulted him and, instead of graduating, served seven months of a one-year jail sentence, using the leisure to study law. Shortly after he was freed, he was admitted to the bar and worked up a successful practice in Bristol, Virginia.

When Virginia seceded, he enlisted in the First Virginia Cavalry, under Colonel Jeb Stuart. He was not a success. With no background in army discipline, he was impatient, bored, and underfoot. Still, the flamboyant Stuart recognized

· · · · · ·

a kindred soul and used him as a scout to gather information on the disposition of the Union troops. He was so good at scouting that Stuart, now a brigadier general, gave him a kind of semidetached command to conduct his own brand of guerrilla warfare, which he invented as he went along.

Mosby and his Rangers were the scourge of the Union. Northern newspapers called him a common horse thief, an outlaw, a spy. One described him as having "infested the Federal skirts like a flea in a beggar's gabardine; he was as pervasive, as annoying, as incurable as the proverbial seven-year's itch." He fought a war of wits that consistently baffled his opponents and entertained his fans, brightening morale in Virginia. Some historians credit Mosby with extending the life of the Confederacy by six months — a dubious glory.

Grant issued orders that anyone who got hold of Mosby or his men was not to take prisoners, simply to hang them from the nearest tree. Even after the war was over, there was a $5,000 bounty on the Mosby head. That was considerable money then, but no one collected.

"The gray ghost," the Union soldiers called him. He had a genius for materializing with a few picked men out of nowhere and vanishing again with Yankee prisoners, guns, and horses.

Not that he was creeping around in camouflage. In fact, he usually wore a billowing scarlet-lined cape and a hat with a huge ostrich-feather plume that curled around over his shoulder. His silhouette on horseback, against the sky on a darkening hilltop, was his trademark. Obviously he was having a wonderful time. He may have been praying for another Hundred Years War.

Off his horse, he was less impressive: a small man with a

slight stoop, he can't have weighed 120 pounds, though they say that his peculiarly luminous and piercing blue eyes commanded instant respect. Nobody sneered at Mosby. And for that matter, he rarely got off his horse. His headquarters were in his saddle; his camps were the homes of friendly Virginians; his men seemed to gather when and where he needed them through a kind of mental telepathy.

He was less interested in bloodshed than in supplies, and in keeping the Federal forces distracted and busy. He roved all around here — some people still call the area Mosby's Confederacy — teasing the Union generals and collecting useful booty. When a Union general called him a horse thief, he retorted that all the stolen horses had had riders, and all the riders had had sabers and pistols. This was not strictly true. Sometimes the riders, complete with sabers and pistols, were asleep, or drunk, or elsewhere, and the horses were just hanging around the stables or tied to trees when they caught Mosby's eye. He was a roving collector of Federal property. Once he collected an entire supply train of 525 wagons.

This unwieldy caravan, a mile and a half long, was trundling from Harpers Ferry to Sheridan's army in Winchester (over the mountain from me) with three thousand men and a herd of cattle bringing up the rear. Mosby usually worked with only a handful of his men, but for this caper he called up all three hundred Rangers. He'd gotten his hands on a couple of pieces of light field artillery, but one gun lost a wheel on the way and had to be abandoned. The other was set up on the Berryville road in what turned out to be a yellow jackets' nest, and they had to move it, with much profanity and horses rearing.

You'd think somebody connected with the wagon train

. . . . . .

would have noticed all this commotion, but nobody did. Most were boiling coffee for breakfast.

Mosby's gun fired a twelve-pounder that knocked the head off a mule. It's probably disconcerting when you're rolling along the peaceful green Shenandoah Valley, ringed by blue mountains, thinking about breakfast, and your mule's head flies off. "The whole train," wrote Ranger John Munson, "stopped and writhed in its center as if a wound had been opened in its vitals."

After a second shot, the Union expedition fell apart: mules, horses, and cattle stampeding; infantry running in all directions; and Mosby riding up and down the line encouraging the confusion. According to Munson, "Then we rushed them ... each man doing his best to out-yell his comrades and emptying revolvers, when we got among them, left and right."

The Rebel yell was probably more effective than the revolvers. The Federal troops were mostly not experienced soldiers but hundred-day men, signed on for specific duties and looking forward to going home. After firing a single volley, an Ohio captain shouted to his men to scatter and save themselves. "Well, we ran," one of them wrote later.

"It was not long before we had the enemy thoroughly demoralized," says Munson, "and were able to turn our attention to the prisoners and the spoils." They unhitched the horses, rifled the wagons, and then burned most of them. (They overlooked the pay wagon, with $112,000 in it. Some accounts say the Yankees came back and collected it the next day, but others hint that a humble Berryville shoemaker "suddenly blossomed out into a man of means, marrying later into one of the best families in the Valley.")

The local people joined in the fun. Sam Moore, a young

. . . . . .

Berryville boy, never forgot the scene and Mosby's Rangers: "They had for us all the glamour of Robin Hood and his merry men," he wrote, "all the courage and bravery of the ancient crusaders, the unexpectedness of benevolent pirates and the stealth of Indians."

With three hundred prisoners, two hundred beef cattle, five or six hundred horses and mules, and "many valuable stores," they headed back toward their home base. "Our captives were on foot," Munson wrote, "while we were mounted, the victors and vanquished chatting freely together...with a song on every man's lips."

Among the booty they'd unearthed a shipment of musical instruments and "the leaders of the mounted vanguard made the morning hideous with attempts to play plantation melodies on the tuneless fiddles." Surrounded by bellowing, neighing, and braying livestock, they "wallowed along in the hot dust of that August morning," and "down the turnpike into the rushing Shenandoah...dashed the whole cavalcade, some swimming, some wading, others finding ferriage at the tail of a horse or steer. The orchestra in the lead scraped away bravely at their fiddles. Only the unhorsing of some of the worst of the performers saved them from bodily violence at the hands of their justly indignant comrades. In a short time, dripping but refreshed, we emerged from the stream, struggled on up the road and began the ascent of the Blue Ridge Mountains." (Up my way, along my road, past where my house stands now.)

Lee surrendered at Appomattox on April 9, 1865, but not Mosby. He stalled. As the Confederate Army disintegrated, more and more stubborn men flocked to the Rangers, until a week before Appomattox he was up to eight hundred and had to form a new company.

He wrote, "I have had no information as yet that would justify my concluding the Confederate cause is altogether hopeless." Grant issued orders to "hunt him and his men down. Guerrillas... will not be entitled to quarter." Most of his Rangers were finally paroled out on April 21, with Mosby shaking each hand; he "cried like a child," one wrote. Then with half-a-dozen holdouts he headed toward Joe Johnston's army, still struggling to the south.

Then Johnston surrendered. On June 29 even John Mosby had to face facts and, with a direct parole from Grant, gave himself up. The party was over.

He lived on till he was eighty-two, lonely and bored. He eventually had eight children, but even that didn't cheer him up. Thirty years after disbanding his men, he said, "I wish that life's descending shadows had fallen upon me in the midst of friends and the scenes I loved best."

Sherman said war was hell, but for Mosby it was more like heaven.

By now, it wouldn't surprise me if some of his Rangers rode creaking and jingling up to the kitchen door and asked for a cup of water.

For those of us here in his stomping grounds, he's a heavenly hero. Let the rest of Virginia revere the gentleman Lee; we have our wild Mosby and what my great-grandfather, marching through here in the wrong-color uniform, called "his merry men." The nine-year-old boy in each of us cherishes the ghost of the Gray Ghost, swooping down from the hills in his plumed hat.

. . . . . .

Not that we have any shrines at which to worship. Only a handful of official roadside markers record his passages through the land. He left us no headquarters to restore, only this rolling land itself, mountain cabins and valley farms, which a few wistful souls would like to have officially designated as Mosby's Confederacy. That should certainly mystify the new people moving into the housing developments, coming from away, bare of memory and myth.

I WENT TO A MEETING of the historical society in a county south of here. After the speeches we milled around the library cuddling cups of punch, brushing cookie crumbs from our shirtfronts, and complaining about the weather and the government.

An elderly, straight-backed gentleman was denouncing both candidates in the recent senatorial election. Pitiful specimens, he said, and a crying shame to the state that called itself "Mother of Presidents" if this was the best we could offer. Having dismantled their characters piece by piece and scorned them equally, he fixed me with a flashing eye and said, "And they aren't either one of them even Virginians. They're both from away."

However foolish or venal they might be, their unforgivable sin was that they were outlanders. Foreigners.

Like me. I nodded guiltily, and presently drifted away to the punch bowl.

I'm adjusting slowly to Virginian patriotism. I lived for years in Maryland and in Pennsylvania and can't recall meeting anyone, however long established, who considered himself first and foremost a Marylander or a Pennsylvanian. Most states are only political concepts, matters of legislators to vote for and taxes to pay. Virginia's different. It always was. Lee wasn't alone in fighting a war for his country and then, forced to choose, choosing Virginia instead, however regretfully. Most Virginians did. There was simply no contest. America was their country, but Virginia was their mother, their home, their heart, the mystic dirt of love. Today's Virginians can think of no prettier name to bestow on their enterprises — Virginia Bar and Grill, Virginia Cleaning Service, Virginia Village Shopping Center.

GENEALOGY IS A MAJOR PASTIME HERE. I'd always sneered at people who rake through the records looking for their family names. I thought they were trying to claim some reflected glory from the rich and famous dead. Maybe, in other places, they are, but here people seem to search for nothing more glorious than a name in the tax records. The *Virginia* tax records.

Each county treasures its records. My own rejoices in a handsome little building maintained for no other purpose than looking up names. Most people here don't need to travel in search of their roots; they can stop off for roots on the way to the supermarket. Find their name. Not wealth or fame or vast acreage, but the bald fact that a man of that name married a Huldah Hawkins in 1803.

This gives them deep satisfaction. The name fastens them to the county they call home in the state that feels like a whole world. They, unlike the senatorial candidates, belong here.

The newspaper runs a regular column listing names and dates. It's very dull. The old records don't show birth dates — being born was a private matter, written into a family Bible

. . . . . .

that was eaten by mice generations ago. Getting married was a public matter. Owning a business was public. We have the records because just before the Yankee troops occupied our county seat in 1862, George K. Fox Jr., clerk of the court, loaded them into a wagon and kept moving them around through southwestern Virginia until the summer of '65, when he brought them all back for us.

We can learn that in 1813 Thomas Brewer operated a mill; Henry Silcott ran an "ordinary" and in 1783 charged so-and-so much for meals, for lodging, for boarding a horse. William Castleman ran the ferry; John Moore billed the sheriff for making handcuffs. Land matters were public: so many acres, such-and-such a plot in the town. A house that was sold in 1769 to George Luckett, who left it to his daughter Sarah, who married Benjamin Virts. Military matters were public. Naturally the ancestors fought in the Civil War, but it's important to know which regiment, which skirmishes, and who was commanding officer. It's all in the records.

HERE, TOO, at this other Virginia county's historical society, the walls are lined with precious records, loved and dusted. With a fresh cup of punch, I sidle over to a corner and pull down some volumes at random. I remember that my grandmother's mother's family had started their American lives in Virginia. After the Civil War they went west and grew — according to the photographs — those rock-ribbed, enduring prairie faces with the wintry mouths, but they started from here.

Newby was the name. I turn the pages, check the indexes. Newby. Sure enough, in 1704 a Nathaniel Newby paid taxes on 850 acres in Nansemond County. In 1716 Henry Newby

· · · · · ·

was a citizen of Maryes White Chappell Parish in Lancaster County. In 1762 in Lancaster County, Whaley Newby married Thos. Pollard. Another Pollard, John, married Lucy Newby in 1819. Nineteen Virginia Newbys fought in the Revolution.

I can't establish a direct line; I can't tell where my great-grandmother fits in. I don't know if this spiderweb is strong enough for the straight-backed gentleman with the flashing eyes, but they were Newbys and Virginians; they were here.

I, too, am here, having traveled across the generations by way of North Carolina; Kansas; Colorado; Washington, D.C.; Maryland; Pennsylvania — a winding road, but I can call myself a Virginian many times removed, and maybe, after all, I am.

I rejoin the milling historical society with my own back a bit straighter, ready to look them all in the eye.

If they want to secede again, they can count on me.

weather report

. . . .

It was a wolf, and it was standing in the lane broadside to my car, and like most easterners, I brake for wolves. Sometimes I even roll up the window.

I could tell it was real by my own reaction, the kind of awe nobody offers a mere dog. Seeing wolves in the zoo, I'd often thought how much they look like German shepherds. Seeing one in the lane, I realized they don't at all.

It ignored my car, standing with its head held high above a magnificent ruff, gazing away toward some invisible distance over which it was king. My sometime-neighbor Jim emerged from the brush in a camouflage coverall, carrying a rifle. "It's okay, he's real gentle," he said. "He was raised with people. His name's Timber. Timber? Come, Timber!" Timber didn't hear him.

"He's yours?"

"Yup. I just got him. I'm going to breed him with Elsa, my shep, and let the pups run free on the mountain." His eyes were shining.

Jim was one of a string of sublessees in the remains of the farmhouse, beyond the overgrown pasture. The owner, my childhood companion Alfred, lives in California. He rents the place to Tom, but Tom shows up only rarely, to work on the boat he's building in the barn. The house he sublets to adventurous friends who come up from the city to play on summer weekends.

Jim was one of these. He'd been there off and on since spring. Jim believed in the free and natural life, which turned out to involve a lot of high-speed travel in an all-terrain vehicle full of shrieking friends. Now he beamed upon Timber like a man who sees his dream made flesh. "Won't it be great," he said, "to have a whole pack of them up here, all living naturally the way they were meant to live?"

The mountain that recently seemed so big and wild seemed suddenly smaller, a tight fit for free-range wolf crosses. Plainly he wasn't planning to feed them; he wasn't often here anyway. They were expected to live off the land. "Do they eat cats?" I asked.

"Cats?" He looked blank; cats aren't part of the wilderness game.

"I have a cat. She's outdoors a lot. Picnic lunch for your wolf pack."

"Oh, cats can climb a tree. No problem," he said, dismissing them with a wave. "Here, Timber!"

Very slowly Timber turned his splendid head and looked at Jim, and through him, and out the other side into non-human spaces. "I have to get to the *store*," I said, and touched the horn. The wolf's pale, daunting gaze considered the car, and then with enormous dignity he moved aside, just enough for me to squeeze past and drive away onto the sane, familiar county road.

Indignation clenched my throat. They think this place is a game, these city pioneers. All summer, on weekends, visitors had gathered at the farmhouse, blocking the lane with cars, and brought what were certainly fully automatic weapons which they fired all day, presumably at the sky, since the steady roar never paused or changed direction.

To Jim and his friends this is Davy Crockett country, Natty Bumppo country, little boy country, the American dream of a wilderness where nobody has to work for a living. No renter has ever planted so much as a tomato here. To them, the mountain means freedom from rules and jobs and women-folk. Freedom to make loud noises, raise wolves, wear cam-ouflage, and pretend to be at war.

I'm insulted for my once-busy mountainside. When I was a summering child here, two milk cows, Rosa and Dolly Varden, surrounded by a squawk of chickens, lived in that barn where Tom's building his boat. Lady and Beauty plowed the half-acre garden that fed the family. Before that it was an apple orchard, marked on the old maps by fluffy green cir-clets. The mountain once worked for a living, and if it's re-verting to forest now, it still has its dignity to be respected. The mountain is not a toy. Our wildlife here is real wildlife, and independent. In November a friend came back from a morning walk around my woods and reported seeing six wild turkeys, a gray fox, a small black bear, and fourteen whitetail deer. Bruce, who hunts my land, says every deer he's killed here had only wild food in its stomach, only natural forest browse, while every deer he's killed in the valley was full of corn and soybeans: civilized deer, parasites. I am obscurely proud of my own because they eat what they ate before the white man came. They're not toys. They *live* here.

A wolf is not a toy either. Apparently Timber's definition of running free was broader than Jim's, and several days later the road and the village below blossomed with signs saying "LOST WOLF — Answers to Timber," and the farmhouse phone number.

The signs faded in the sun and warped in the fall rains. I studied the local papers for reports of devastated henhouses and frightened children, but all was silence. Northern Virginia had swallowed a full-grown timber wolf as easily as if he'd been a squirrel.

Then I passed a U-Haul parked at the farmhouse, and I haven't seen Jim around since. Winter's coming, and the mountain in winter is grown-up country.

THE WINTER WAS A HARD ONE, and toward spring reports came up from the village of two dogs and several sheep being savaged and killed by what, from a distance, looked like an enormous gray German shepherd. After that I heard no more.

WINTER NIGHTS ARE QUIET on the mountain. Except when the wind whines, sleet rattles, an owl calls, or a branch cracks under its load of ice, the quiet is so intense I can hear the cat breathing.

Living here, I've lost my tolerance for the songs of civilization. I shrink from the sounds of truck tires, hair dryers, television laugh tracks, beepers, microwaves, sirens. The purr of the refrigerator is an intrusion; I've stopped using the vacuum cleaner and sweep the floor with a broom.

· · · · · ·

Still, I need to hear *something*, if just to remind me that my ears work. I've lost the knack of watching television, now that I need it badly. It's come to seem alternately foolish and bullying, and always an alien presence on the mountain.

In the short winter daylight I can hear a chain saw or a dog barking, sometimes a blue jay, sometimes the ice in the trees rattling like bones, but at night the silence is so complete it circles around and turns into something like a sound, a song I could understand if I listened long enough.

I can almost hear my neighbors packing to leave. C. J. and his wife, originally from far to the south, vowed last March never to spend another winter here. The Silcotts, on the other side of the mountain, totaled two cars and watched part of their roof collapse last February under the ice; they too are packing up.

No tire tracks will mark their lanes this year, leaving a friendly footprint, like Friday's, in the snow.

In the city and the suburbs, it's no great matter to go outside, where night is almost as bright as the living room, but the blinding darkness of the mountain at six on a December evening seals me home by the lamps.

In my possibly flawed memory, city winters were unobtrusive, city snows harmless, and gaily dressed citizens strolled from party to party laughing and caroling.

I invoke my foremothers in Kansas and Colorado, isolated for months in two-room cabins full of woodsmoke and crying children. Closer and more recently, down in my valley, until half a century ago, nobody struggled to get out in the winter. The lanes drifted shut and the people stayed home. They wore a path to the barn and the woodpile and stayed home with a cellarful of food, eggs and milk and butter ready to hand, and got on with their winter chores, mending clothes and machinery, carrying water to the livestock, pitching down forkfuls of hay from the loft. With plenty to eat and plenty of work to do, who needed the world? The only reason to get out was to fetch a doctor for impending births and deaths. How did we get so decentralized that winter travel turned compulsory, even for country folk?

Storms here come in from the west, hit the ridge, and detonate, then fizzle out gently on their way to the eastern cities. The rare coastal storm slams in from the east, bangs its head on the mountains, and hangs pinioned there struggling fiercely for three days.

Even with C. J. and his family gone, I'm not entirely alone. Other people live along the county road as it slopes down to the Gap. Driving, with the leaves off the trees, I can see houses. I don't know those people, though, and probably never will. I can hardly ask strangers to come jump-start my car, or call them from the valley to see if the plow went through or the power's still on. They won't, in a crisis, feed my cats and my birds and my woodstove. I don't even know their names. Whatever sounds they make never scratch the silence here.

The other seasons have their companionable night music. At the ragged tail end of winter, as soon as the porch thermometer creeps above freezing, the peepers start to sing in the woods, the most welcome sound of the country year, thin as a grass blade, clear as air, the music springwater would make if it had a voice. I never see a peeper, the tiny green tree frog no bigger than my thumb, but I strain my ears to gulp in as much of his sound as I can, rejoicing: spring will come.

. . . . . .

Then the pond down the hill thaws and the big frogs sign on with resonant, dignified burps. The leaves on the maple tree open and rustle. Birds shorten the night. Towhees, loud and territorial, are the first awake, just as dawn grays the windows. "Drink your tea!" they insist. "Drink your teee-ea!" They wake the other birds, and long before sunrise my bedroom rings with cries of "Teacher, teacher!" "Cheerfully, cheerfully!" "Judy? Judy?" and "Wheateater, wheateater, wheateater, wheat!"

Summer moves in, the birds quiet down, and the bugs take over. On a hot night in August the air is a solid wall of cicada-shout. They seem to operate, not as individual solos, but in congregations, nearer cicadas and farther cicadas, question and answer, call and echo: *Shout!* ("shout"); *Shout!* ("shout"). Thunderstorms rattle and flash in the dark, and I get up to close the windows. Violent bangs send a timid cat down to hide in the basement, not to return till morning, smelling of mildew, whiskers full of cobwebs.

The dark turns chilly and abruptly, between one night and the next, the cicadas hush and the crickets chime in, warning hysterically of frost, as if winter were something we could stop in its tracks if only we caught it in time.

Frost comes. The crickets perish, all except the one somewhere deep in a closet, singing alone, possibly having found something delicious to eat, maybe a patchwork quilt; crickets are unaccountably fond of quilts, especially antique quilts. He's almost welcome to it, though, in return for his companionable song. Then he, too, falls silent. Winter is here. My ears ache with paying attention, straining to hear trees dreaming, foxes walking, stars wheeling, rocks thinking.

———

MY CHILDREN ARE reluctant to come for Christmas, considering the prospect of having to stay till April, carrying stovewood and playing endless games of Scrabble and Monopoly in the cold gray light of snow.

At least this year I'm braced for it.

The new woodstove crouches in the basement as if to spring, an environmentally correct stove equipped with all the latest bells and whistles. I acquired it at dizzying expense from a certified woodstove specialist, and its operating instructions look like the instructions you get when you buy the Concorde.

I'm calling it Sophie to try to humanize it.

There's wood enough for a month, cat food enough for a week, sunflower seeds, at the rate they're going, for about an hour. Oil in the lamps, soup in the cupboard to warm on Sophie. A bucket of water for flushing the toilet, a kettle of water for tea. Calm, philosophical people, thus armed against cold and hunger and the inevitable power failure, would settle down with the works of Dickens and wait contented for spring.

For me, the raging claustrophobe, this is fine for the first day, though I have trouble getting into *Martin Chuzzlewit*. The second day, I pace. I'm perfectly comfortable here — *but I can't get out.* My home is an elevator trapped between floors; I pound on the walls and howl.

After one apocalyptic storm, both doors were drifted shut. I climbed out onto the deck through a window, crawled under the railing, and dropped down into the snow. With my hands and a fallen branch I poked enough snow from the porch screen door to squeeze in through it and get a shovel. I waded up the slope and shoveled the kitchen door free and walked triumphantly in through it. I couldn't *go* anywhere, of course, but at least I could get the *door* open; at least I wasn't bottled up in there scratching my initials on the dungeon walls and making friends with rats.

Later I realized I might have broken my ankle and had to set it myself, since the rescue squad doesn't own a helicopter.

The phone still works. Friends call. City friends are baffled. "What do you mean, snowed in? Why don't you just call a plowing service?"

"There isn't any."

Here on the mountain, folks do their own plowing. This is not a service-oriented world, and even the frail and elderly do their chores with only minimal aid from younger relatives or helpful neighbors. We cut our own lawns, our own wood, our own hair. We bolt a plow blade to our pickup and plow our own lanes.

"Plow" is too strong a word. In my city days, I considered a plowed street to be one you could cross wearing ordinary shoes. Around here, it's called "breaking open," instead, as in "Harrison came over on his tractor and broke it open." This means it's shallower than it was, and a heavy vehicle with four-wheel drive can wallow carefully out to the blacktop.

I call for help.

A woman at the newspaper who lives over on the north mountain says her daddy has a plow, but he only plows for neighbors because it isn't road legal and doesn't have plates. Another friend knows the number of a man in the valley with a backhoe; he charges an arm and a leg, but it's worth it if I need to get out.

Well, I suppose I don't *need* to get out. There's still soup, still cat food. *I just want to.* Just to see some faces. Get down

· · · · · ·

off the mountain. *Anywhere.* Just for an hour. Or even just as far as the county road, to know it can be done. Dimly I try to remember the name of a woman, some miscreant in Imperial Rome, who was exiled to quite a small island and immediately went raving mad and had to be chained.

I call the number. No answer. He's off somewhere on his backhoe, charging an arm and a leg. There's Harrison, but C. J.'s wife has told me firmly, "You don't *call* for Harrison, you *pray* for Harrison." Harrison is a native here, descendant of many of the earliest settlers, and you don't push him around, saying, "Harrison, do this, do that." When and if the spirit moves him, Harrison will come.

I abandon prayer and call anyway. His wife answers. He was out breaking folks open for eighteen hours and now, too tired for safety, has gone to bed. She takes my number. Maybe tomorrow, maybe Thursday.

The first jagged edges of panic flicker in the corners of the room.

If I had the sense of a gnat, I'd have left the car up by the road, within shoveling distance of the county plow. Along the roads, all winter, cars and pickups sit empty at the ends of lanes, and behind them many footprints, coming and going, mark the way home through woods and fields. "Walking in," it's called: "We've been walking in for a week now."

My car, however, is here, where for transportation purposes it might as well be a tree.

I feed the stove, light the lamps, and walk from bookcase to bedroom door and back to bookcase. I reflect bitterly on friends I used to have who collected oil lamps as ornaments. Antiques. Decor. Groping in the kitchen's bosky gloom, I set my sandwich down in a puddle of lamp oil but don't notice

· · · · · ·

until I've taken the first bite. I turn on the radio, foresightedly furnished with batteries, but the news comes from the city. In the city the dusting of snow has melted. Besides, whatever the crisis, in the city "they" will do something. "They" will take care of you, however tardily, and all the citizen needs to do is wait and complain. Here, "they" is us.

It's important not to panic. It's important to keep busy.

I fill a pitcher with sunflower seeds, put on my boots, and squeeze through the snowdrifted storm door onto the deck.

There's no moon. Far below the lights of cars move freely through the plowed world. And over my head, stars.

There's Polaris in Ursa Minor, pointing the way north. And southward over the valley, that's Orion. I haven't seen Orion in ages, but there he is, unmistakably, immensely himself, the stars of his belt hanging close enough to pick like apples. My prison cell opens to include Andromeda, Cassiopeia, and the Pleiades.

It's cold out here and the snow is over my boots, but there's all that sky up there. The panic begins to drain from my shoulders. I fill the bird feeder and take long stinging breaths of starry cold and space.

Everything will be all right. Harrison will come, or, if not Harrison, then spring.

NOVEMBER 11—Five inches of snow slammed rock hard by eighty-mile-an-hour winds. Several large trees crashed, one across the side yard where I often park my car, though happily not last night.

NOVEMBER 14—Snow all night and all day for a total of nineteen inches.

. . . . . .

NOVEMBER 16—Plowed out, I drive around giddy with freedom. Deep snow on ground not yet frozen; here and there a thrifty farmer is turning it under for the nitrogen.

NOVEMBER 27—Rejoicing. Brown patches appear in snow cover, and I rush out to start the fall chores. Clean gutters; bring in garden hose, deck furniture, hammock; gather kindling. Catch myself inspecting brown patches for signs of crocuses and snowdrops; surely spring almost here? Cold wind springs up, abandon plans to rake leaves.

NOVEMBER 28—Five more inches of snow, nailing down a blanket of plastered, sodden oak leaves. The lawn, as "lawn," is history. When the fog starts to lift, I can see green fields in the valley, but the weatherman says it may get down to ten degrees tonight, meaning zero on the mountain. What a long winter it's going to be.

THE POSTMISTRESS REMEMBERS the blizzard of '66, when they had to use dynamite on the twenty-foot drifts in the roads and the dairymen poured their milk out into the snow for a week because the trucks couldn't get through to collect it. Winters are part of our social glue here; everywhere people gather, they reminisce and compare. A long accumulation of remembered winters is a badge of belonging, and I, who wasn't here in '66, must make do with the ice of '94, the floods of '96.

A friend, a Virginia transplant from New England, writes to say that in Virginia the official reaction to snow is that the Lord sent it, and when the Lord's good and ready he'll take it away.

The children have decided not to come for Christmas.

IT'S A SUMMER RETREAT, this house, built for the enjoyment of pleasant weather. A house without a furnace, almost without insulation, so that north winds blow through the walls. A house designed to leave its doors and windows open day and night and then, after the last bright leaf has fallen, to have its pipes drained and be left alone with its thoughts till April, part of the mountain, like a snow-covered rock. I have violated its winter privacy, and in return it makes no effort to feel like shelter or lull me into thinking man has conquered winter. A summer house in winter is like a beach house when it never stops raining.

This time of year I sometimes think a bit wistfully of my city days. Not just the glorious convenience of plowed streets and shoveled sidewalks, friends to visit, streetlights winking on as the offices empty, but the comfortable sense of being indoors. Sheltered. After I'd pulled off my boots and bolted the door, I was *in*. Winter shrank back beyond the walls, irrelevant, harmless, invisible. My house didn't notice the time of year. Neither did my office; it didn't even have a window.

Everything has its price, and the mountain has sent its bill collector. The wind whines disagreeably and filters through the walls to ruffle my papers. Dark pours in through the curtains. All right, I understand. This is on account of mornings drinking coffee suspended over the green valley; on account of a houseful of violets and goldfinches. It wouldn't be fair not to pay.

At the kitchen sink, pouring coffee, I look out the window at a scarlet cardinal in a dogwood tree loaded with scarlet berries; every twig and crotch holds a cup of feathery snow. Even the worst days on the mountain do have their Hallmark moments. When the sun dips under the ridge behind me, the

· · · · · ·

sky overhead turns mother-of-pearl and the valley and the sky above it turn mauve and then briefly pink before dark swallows them all. The January Wolf Moon and February Hunger Moon lay fine purple tree shadows across the snow.

I defrost some of my own personal peaches and raspberries and eat them slowly; they go straight to the bloodstream with messages of hope. The dogwood scratches on the window in the wind. Its twigs are tipped with buds, bulging, gray, purse-folded, and encased in perfect globes of ice. The buds have been there since summer, waiting confidently.

Dogwoods are great optimists. Daffodils wait and see, crouching firmly underground just in case spring doesn't come this year, but dogwoods have faith.

LATE IN EVERY WINTER, bored with confinement, depressed by the apparent permanence of mountain snow, I am seized by a flurry of domestic energy. This is what psychologists call "displacement activity," meaning that what I really want to do is go outside and rake the mulch off the raspberries and look for hepaticas in the woods.

Last year I painted the living room and wrenched my back moving file cabinets. The year before I took all fifty thousand books off their accustomed shelves and piled them everywhere, arranged them by category or author's last initial, and put them back in new, logical places and now I can't find anything I need. The year before that I stripped all the furniture, making myself sick as a dog with the fumes, and sanded and oiled it.

The fit usually strikes in the evening, after a long day's writing, when every muscle cries aloud for employment, and a project once in motion is hard to stop, so midnight often finds me balanced on a kitchen chair with a mouthful of nails.

This is the year of the basement.

My mother designed the house, and she wanted a really big deck. Quite rightly so; it's the summer living room, dining room, and office, with space for a potted vegetable garden, hammock, chairs, barbecue, and many bird feeders. It does, however, hang out a long way over the basement. She put generous east-facing windows down there, probably hoping the morning sun would shine in, and for all I know it does, maybe for five minutes in the middle of June, but I have better things to do on June mornings than hang out in the basement waiting to check. The rest of the time the place is as dark as a bat's belly. Look out the windows, past the wood-piles and wheelbarrow and rusty shovels, and even the most brilliant day, the kind of day that could strike you snow-blind, seems remote as the light at the end of the Channel Tunnel.

For reasons known only to herself, Mother painted the walls the exact color of a month-old mushroom forgotten in the bottom of the refrigerator. Few basements are jolly places to hang out, but this one feels like a kind of hideous exile from the world of the living, such as might happen to a princess kidnapped by dragons. Even a brief dash down to feed the woodstove and take its temperature makes me want to cry.

I am painting it white. In my mind's eye this will cheer it up enormously, but my mind's eye fails to note the stained gray concrete floor deep in wood litter from feeding the stove and splotched with ancient stains, probably cat related. It ignores the layers of boxes in the storage room, left by siblings over the decades and now rotted into compost around the unidentifiable mildewed or rusted treasures they once held.

My mind's eye struggles to remain hopeful enough to finish the job.

Finishing these winter jobs can be a problem. They have their built-in deadline. One day I'll wander over to the window, paintbrush in hand, and see spring creeping up the east face of the mountain, tree by tree, like a slow, greenish yellow sunrise, and that will be that. Chairs and tables will remain huddled in the middle of the room, topped by the roller pan, and the original mushroom gray will still scowl through the first sloppy coat of white. Who needs a cheerful basement, or even a house, in the spring?

"You must have had quite the winter up there on the mountain," says Mrs. General Store, ringing up my eggs and newspaper.

I don't know her name. I think of her and her husband as part of their overstuffed little store, rather than as people. I have never seen either of them anywhere else. Perhaps, like trolls in the sunlight, they'd disintegrate if they stepped outside.

"We sure did."

Mountain folk get considerable respect in the valley for wintering up there, and we earn it. I'm still dizzy at the ease of being down in North Hill; at having so thoughtlessly jumped into my car and driven down, my lane now rutted mud instead of glacier. I still marvel at coming to the store for things I could live without.

Winter exposes a number of once-essential items as superfluous. Almost everything, in fact, except cat food, toilet paper, and coffee. Winter classifies the Sunday paper as a luxury. For me, anyway. It's different for men.

· · · · · ·

Regularly they risk their lives and their precious vehicles to drive to the general store for a cup of coffee, a newspaper, a doughnut. They swagger in the narrow aisles, flaunting the frivolousness of the trip, pretending they never noticed the snow-deep roads glazed with fresh ice. "Have any trouble getting out?" they ask each other, and lie: "Trouble? No, no trouble."

Attendance is taken. "Bill been in?" "Haven't seen him." Bill's manhood is on the line, and he'll hear about it if he couldn't get out or, worse, didn't even try, but stayed warm and safe at home with his own coffeepot instead of the store's Styrofoam cup.

There are always more men here than women. The women drive sensibly to the faceless supermarket in the next town over, buy what they need, and go home. The men come to the general store. They check in with each other in a word or two or a nod. They loiter. Home and family are all very well, but this store represents community, and no man wants to be an island. City folk touch base in their offices, fitting themselves into place in the world. Here, without offices, we use the general store. I pick up scraps of talk: "... so I put it under the hay cart to keep dry, but that was August, when it never rained at all..." "... figured he killed her fair and square, so he slings her over his shoulder, and darned if that bobcat didn't come alive on him..."

This store seems to be staying afloat, but I worry about it. Every village in the valley, sometimes only a crossroads, used to have its store, some going back for generations in the same family. Every couple of years now, another one closes. Once they offered almost everything anyone needed, but now the post offices have moved to separate quarters and the single

. . . . . .

gas pump, always a nuisance for the suppliers, has vanished. Now some of the old stores display weathering For Sale signs out front, next to the posters saying "Game-Weighing Station" and "Potluck Dinner at the First Baptist Church. Bring a Dish to Share."

It's a public service, keeping open these gentle little clubs where neighbors meet, run a tab, pass the news, and buy a six-pack or a can of tuna; serious shopping goes elsewhere, and the money here must be small, the hours are brutal, and surely nobody's sons and daughters want to take over, any more than they wanted the dairy farms. Mrs. General Store looks well past retirement age. Her husband raises ducks for extra cash, but at the prices he's been getting, he says he might as well eat them himself. Someday they will simply fade back into the jumble of rabbit pellets, jackknives, potato chips, chewing tobacco, sinus remedies, canned soup, pruning shears, and Dr. Pepper.

In summer the general store loses its private solidarity. Souvenir T-shirts bloom from the ceiling and strangers on bicycles stop in for Gatorade. Sometimes adventurous families with out-of-state tags drive up, all wearing merrily patterned shorts, as if North Hill were a cruise ship, and exclaim at our nameless little store that sags so quaintly on its foundations.

When the weather improves, it's no longer a point of pride for the local men to stop in every morning, and besides, they're busy now. In the quiet afternoons Mr. or Mrs. General Store will sit motionless on a stool behind the counter and stare at a black-and-white television, gradually getting older.

Without our stores, the villages would feel as meaningless as a suburb and the scattered farms would have no center. Churches and volunteer fire departments don't lend them-

. . . . . .

selves to hanging out, not without an official reason. The post office always presents a chance to chat, but no coffee as an excuse to linger. When the stores are gone, how will we know who we are, or where, or whether we still have neighbors?

In an anxious gesture of support, I buy a bag of cookies and some flashlight batteries I no longer need and go out through the enclosed porch, where snow shovels have been replaced by rakes and garden hoses, rock salt by fertilizer.

It *is* spring, after all, and maybe winter will never come back. Maybe birds will always sing, the sun always shine, and shabby old general stores endure forever, their freezer chests dripping, floors creaking, drawing us in from far and wide to remind us we aren't alone.

SPRING ON THE MOUNTAIN is a gradual matter and subject to frequent setbacks that bury the daffodils under a foot of snow, but as it progresses I begin to feel less helpless, better able to cope with whatever curves the mountain throws me. I'm not, but it's the thought that counts.

The cats go out to reclaim their world. One of them kills a squirrel and brings it home. Poor devil; for this he clung to life all winter and managed to survive?

In the valley, spring is already entrenched. Down at the diner, the men stretch out their mud-boots under the big back table while the waitress circles them pouring more black coffee into their mugs. Their talk has gone back to politics, gossip, and tractors.

I can make a dentist appointment. Get a haircut. It's over.

The month of May is called merry for many excellent reasons, not least of them being that now I can stop thinking about the weather. I can put the almanacs away. Stop

· · · · · ·

channel-surfing the evening news, shopping around for the best deal in forecasts. For the next six months I can take the weather for granted. Enjoy it or ignore it.

In May, I can get down on my knees and grope in the back of the sacred emergency cupboard, drag out the bottle of twelve-year-old Scotch from behind the soup and cat food and candles, and open it. I can toss the last of the wood on the fire just to brighten a foggy evening.

For months it has seemed like pure masochism to live where I live; now it begins to make sense again. Refreshing waves of sanity sweep over me. Plucking kindling from the melting snow in the woods, I surprise myself singing the grand anthems of my earliest childhood, like "Found a Peanut" and "Mary Ann McCarthy, She Went out to Gather Clams." Surely all I need for perfect happiness is a sturdier, taller car and perhaps winter quarters for a month or even two, a place to repair to where something moves besides chickadees and cardinals, and other voices besides my own can be heard.

Brooding about weather, present or imminent, ate into work time and playtime. It was a bore, all that brooding. Weighing the omens and portents, the almanac, the woolly bear, the groundhog.

I'm skeptical about almanacs myself and recklessly ignore even their advice on planting carrots during the waning moon. An almanac's prediction is man-made; what would mere people know? Surely the creatures who live out there with the weather must have better information. I used to believe in woolly bears — they were dead right in 1978, if you remember *that* one. Unfortunately they blew it last year. A person hardly knows whom to believe anymore. Certainly not groundhogs. Anyone who has ever seen a groundhog by the

· · · · · ·

side of the road, waiting until you're almost upon him before he ambles into your path, must doubt he knows much about spring or anything else.

There's the thickness, they say, of the squirrels' fur, and last fall in my anxiety I actually stopped the car to inspect a road-killed squirrel. It was lovely fur, dense and soft, but was it deeper than usual? What's usual, squirrel-wise?

Some swear by the size of the acorn crop, as if oak trees, in their natural kindness, produce generously to feed the wild-life over a hard winter. (This one I checked out. It isn't true.)

Some of us believe hard winters and mild ones alternate in a kind of celestial evenhandedness; others claim they come in clusters, so that if last year was bad, this year may be worse. The postmistress, who claims she doesn't mind winters, says we've just entered a ten-year cycle of terrible ones. Most of us, irrationally, believe in a kind of quota system, with a certain amount of beastliness allocated to each year: if we don't get it now, we'll get it later. Pleasant weather is a snare, a trap to lure us into spending our stovewood recklessly and eating our emergency soup before trouble slams into us and catches us with our long johns down.

"We'll pay for this," we tell each other darkly, resisting the winter sunshine. "You wait and see. Remember, it's not over till it's over."

In May, it's over.

collectors' items

· · · · · · · · · · · · · · · ·

Friends and relations clean out their closets and bring me their old clothes. Clothes too good for the trash but too shabby to wear — too shabby for my friends, that is, but Barbara can wear them on the mountain, they tell themselves, where only the deer and rabbits will notice the coffee stain, the moth hole, the frayed cuff.

My house bulges with clothes. In my mind, though not in my closets, they fall into several geographic categories on a map marked with concentric circles. The choice of acceptable garments narrows as the circles widen toward civilization and gets complicated by winters, which include November and March, when I can't get as far as the car except dressed as a Muscovite charwoman, booted and bundled and scarved, and emerge in the mild valley from my snow-caked car like a messenger of doom from the frozen north.

The largest clothing category — the fashion-conscious might call it the sole category — is at the center: Mountain Only. These are barely suitable for accepting a package from

United Parcel Service. Blotched and faded, buttons dangling, strings trailing, zippers permanently derailed, they may scandalize even the deer, always impeccable in form-fitting russet fur. In the spring, the gardening jeans, which are also the painting jeans, get muddy and stay muddy, hooked at night over a doorknob; why waste the soap to wash them?

Sometimes, in an absentminded daze, I find myself at the supermarket wearing Mountain Only, but I try to check before getting into my car.

The second circle includes the smallest, closest village and clothes that, though threadbare, cover me decently. To this village I may even wear shorts in summer, though not the Mountain-Only shorts with their grass-stained backsides. Here in North Hill I can mail a letter, get the oil changed, and buy a Sunday paper at the general store. At the general store I can also stock up on lottery tickets, fishhooks, Zippo lighters, pocket watches, pickled eggs, night crawlers, chewing tobacco, lubricating oil for the chain-saw blade, beer, Alka-Seltzer, drill bits, wooden clothespins, and cotton work gloves sized for grizzly bears. For basic groceries, though, I have to move to circle three.

In this more easterly town, a proper town with a traffic light and a Chinese restaurant, I can also visit a dentist, buy a bottle of Scotch or a bunch of flowers, and fill a prescription. Here I never wear shorts (except, as noted, by accident). In winter I check to make sure long underwear isn't dribbling out at wrist and ankle. I comb my hair.

Circle four covers sophisticated destinations like the bank, office supplies, and my job at the newspaper. Here sits the county seat, old and perhaps itself a bit frayed at the cuffs, but eminently respectable. Respectability, not fashion, is the goal here; I have only one pair of wool slacks and two of jeans that qualify. Even the dawdling groups around the high school are respectably dressed, though perhaps they simply have no place to buy the rebellious T-shirts and strange trousers of the urban young.

Here only lawyers wear suits, and the only female suit I've seen was on a young woman headed toward the courthouse with a briefcase. It was a wonderful suit, black, short-skirted, perfectly tailored, matching her perfectly tailored hair. There was something shocking about her, though, and I wasn't the only person to stop on the sidewalk and stare; she couldn't have seemed more out of place if she'd been climbing down from a flying saucer, and it isn't nice to look shocking. Maybe next time she'll know to wear a calf-length print dress and Reeboks.

Circle five contains the cities. Here the clothes dwindle down to a precious few.

My city garments have followed me. My office wardrobe hangs in the damp basement closet, gathering mildew, or lies down in darkness in an old pine chest. Every spring and every fall I move the closet clothes into the chest and the chest clothes into the closet, following a seasonal ritual left over from city life, when the movement of clothes was the primary sign that spring was here or summer was over.

On the increasingly rare occasions when the cities summon me, I spend a long, bewildered time leafing through these old friends before I choose something, give its wrinkles a shake, wonder whatever happened to the iron, dress, and set forth. Later, on the street, I catch sight of myself in a store window and blush. I'm not sure quite why, but I definitely don't look like everyone else. Shoe polish, like nail polish, has slipped out of my life, and I forgot to check for cat hairs before I left. Furthermore, I smell funny. A pervasive, unmistakable scent of mildew shadows me. King Tut probably smells like that. And Dracula.

The last time I had urban business, I rooted under the assorted boots for the good black pumps and hauled them out. They were stuffed with cobwebs. Not fresh, crisp spiderwebs but an ancient lacework spun by the remotest ancestors of any living spider. Under the fuzz, in the toes, mice had stored a handful of cat chow.

Someday I'll just give up. Drape myself in Mountain Only, stay home, and become a famous hermit.

Or, I suppose, I could throw it all away and start over from scratch, but throwing things away here isn't easy. Things accumulate.

IN CIVILIZED AREAS, "trash collection" means that someone comes and takes your trash away. Here, it describes what's in the basement. The shed. The closets.

My basement is gradually filling up. A rising tide of broken deck chairs, mildewed mattresses, and empty paint cans will, in the fairly near future, come surging up the stairs and into the kitchen. The living room. Today, the basement; tomorrow, the world.

Empty milk cartons and junk mail fit easily into plastic trash bags. When I have six of these filled, I load them into my very small car and drive them to the dump, officially the sanitary landfill, and heave them over my head and into a Dumpster parked there for the convenience of what they call "homeowners." Only twice have I lost my grip on the bag and exploded an avalanche of used kitty litter over my head

· · · · · ·

and shoulders. The round-trip to the dump is just under sixty miles, though in full summer when the garbage gets ripe it seems longer.

Newspapers, cans, and bottles go to be recycled in noisy metal containers, off what used to be the main road, behind an old house. It's a good place for a house, and a good house, a foursquare farmhouse with a big porch and a few shutters left at its broken windows. The door is covered with plywood and a bent metal sign tells me it's private property, keep out. Why am I dumping my cans and bottles in its backyard? Where did its people go? Why doesn't anyone want it? Years have gone by and nobody has come for it, nobody buys a secondhand house anymore. I heave my newspapers into Newspapers Only and leave feeling guilty, as after a trip to the animal shelter.

These journeys leave a lot of things unaccounted for. Anyone who has ever tried to cram a mouse-nibbled box spring, a dead lawnmower, or a rusted-out wheelbarrow into a trash bag will understand. Anyone who has struggled to subdue and package the stiffly writhing coils of a forty-foot garden hose, its couplings run over on the driveway once too often, will understand.

In the country, it has always been a hallmark of respectability to keep these things out of sight. A well-run farm has a pit close to the house for pork-chop bones and farther away, preferably behind the barn or off in the woodlot, a larger container, probably a washed-out gully or ravine, final resting place of grandpa's easy chair, rolls of rotted carpet, a former washing machine, bits of Volkswagen.

Nice people keep them hidden.

Folks around here try to stay abreast of the thing tide by

· · · · · ·

having yard sales, often quite shamelessly. Certainly the prices are right; the sellers' motive is not so much financial gain as avoiding a trip to the dump. Everything is arranged neatly on tables, the cracked cups and cupless saucers, spoons rescued too late from the garbage grinder, broken toys, forlorn garments mapped with ancient stains.

Perhaps another motive is purely social, since yard sales are always well attended. People come to chat. The women pick through scraps of plastic kitchen and dining accessories; the men scrabble in cartons of rusty tools, perhaps coming up triumphant with a ten-cent hammer, though they already own a dozen hammers. Men here have trouble resisting the siren song of tools, any tools.

At the end of the day the residue is packed up again and brought inside to wait for the rummage sales.

After all, it isn't quite trash, not yet. It's still *stuff*. It might even come in handy.

We don't throw things away lightly; you never know what you're going to need some day.

We're conservative by nature, too, and slow to toss out the old ways, especially if the new ways cost money. The ancestral German and Scots-Irish farmers in the north valley were still planting their cornfields with a hoe a full generation after the arrival of the iron plow blade. If what we've got still works, we keep using it until it stops working. Then we put it in the attic.

We live in houses, not apartments, so getting rid of accumulated consumer goods isn't the immediate question of survival that it would be in Manhattan. Many of us have barns, toolsheds, chicken houses, and nameless outbuildings of long-forgotten purpose, all begging to be filled with the toys our

· · · · · ·

children once played with and appliances that once served us so well. If you looked back behind the appliances, you'd find withered scraps of horse harness and a disk harrow dissolving into its own rust, though the fields have grown up into full-sized forests since last these left the barn. It's a cozy feeling, our past gathered warmly around us in case we should need it again.

THRIFTY AS WE ARE, we're also generous, and when a worthy cause calls we'll donate a few select treasures.

The North Hill Volunteer Fire and Rescue is a worthy cause. We love our volunteers, and so we should. We hope never to need the various services in which they're certified ("Agricultural-Machinery Extrication" is my own least-favorite) and we write them checks in the same placatory spirit as throwing a virgin down the volcano.

Up the road, behind the Short Hills, the firefighters raise money for a new truck with a benefit baseball game against the sheriff's department in which players must pitch, catch, bat, and run the bases mounted on burros. Over in the county seat the gallant volunteers stage a "Womanless Fashion Show," with firefighters posing in borrowed dresses. In North Hill, however, we maintain our dignity.

Every spring the ladies' auxiliary holds a fund-raising rummage sale, and we grope through our attics and part with something we've been keeping around in case of need. Some neighbor of ours will buy it and keep it around in case of need. The middlemen will buy new tires for their ambulance. All of us will try not to think of the shadow that hangs over the volunteers, the thousands of new houses poised to spring up all around us, just as flammable as the old houses and

· · · · · ·

containing nobody with the time or the conscience to volunteer.

The big day rolls around. The fire trucks are banished to the Methodists' parking lot and the firehouse is a roiling sea of offerings. Furniture sits out front on the apron where the trucks get washed: beanbag chairs from the '70s, butterfly chairs from the '50s. A dinette table in gilt-flecked aquamarine formica. Wooden bedsteads lashed to their wire-coil springs. Television sets the size of holstein cows, with screens you could hide under your hand. Several sewing machines and two cartons of curtain and upholstery material; I can feel in my bones the creative, nest-building urge that bought these things, and the urge's gradual fading that left them behind, washed up on the beach of inertia.

Large appliances stand along the left, labeled either "Works" or "Doesn't Work." Men here like to tinker, and a broken washing machine coaxed back into usefulness brings a rush of satisfaction never to be wrung from a retail purchase.

The main room, sometimes grandly called the fire hall, where wedding receptions are often held, is jammed with long tables, customers, *stuff.* I pick my way past portable Remington typewriters with their keys fused and suitcases with flopping latches to the table of kitchen goods. Someone has bought the waffle iron I donated, but there are others, hinges awry, splotched with the baked-on memories of bygone breakfasts. My past rises up and quivers over the electric hot trays and bun warmers and fondue makers and the cheerful yellow yogurt cookers in which good mothers, in 1968, brewed up homemade yogurt to force down their kids. There are covered cake stands and Drip-O-Later coffeepots and a doughnut fryer shaped in a figure eight, with room for two doughnuts to

. . . . . .

sizzle in oil side by side. And surely I, too, once owned a wok, just as unscrubbably sticky as this one? Whatever happened to my wok? My youth?

Free-form ceramic ashtrays. Wire birdcages. Fluted candy dishes. It occurs to me that some of these items may have seen the inside of the fire hall before, maybe two or three times. Here at the end of the table, flanked by tall black electric fans, is a box of paper patterns, size twelve, for making dresses exactly like those Jacqueline Kennedy wore in a time when surely the winters weren't as cold and spring came earlier than it does today.

Under the tables and stretching the length of the room are cartons of phonograph records: *Sing Along with Mitch* — Mitch Miller and the Gang; *World's Great Love Songs* from the Longines Symphonette Society's Family Library of Beautiful Listening. Someone here in the valley or up on the ridge has kept these for what? fifty years? in case they came in handy. In case the family miraculously reassembled to sing along, or gathered again in the parlor for beautiful listening.

This is no funeral pyre, though; this isn't the landfill. People are buying these things. It's a happy crowd, here in our backwater shopping mall, eagerly rummaging through their neighbors' old boots and shoes, holding up shirts and jackets to their chests, and there's a long line at the cash table. If the original owners have given up on the usefulness of yogurt makers and Mitch Miller, new owners will take them in, recycling someone else's past, keeping it alive, waiting for it to come in handy.

Similar things can be found in flea markets, presented as merchandise, curios, even antiques, but this isn't a flea market. These things are, or were, *ours*. When sold, they'll travel only as far as the barns and attics visible from their original kitchen windows.

An acquaintance beams at me like Christmas morning, his arms overflowing with complicated chunks of greasy metal that, to my ignorant eye, all look vaguely like carburetors. "We were on our way to Winchester," he says, "and saw the sign and stopped off. Looks like we won't ever get to Winchester, not today."

I squeeze over to the book table. Secondhand books don't bring on fits of wistfulness like secondhand bun warmers and turquoise plastic coffee cups; it's right and proper for a book to have many owners and retain its dignity into extreme old age.

Here's the owner's manual for a 1979 Oldsmobile. Did the venerable Olds recently dodder off on its last journey? No matter; the handbook's in good shape and someone will probably buy it and keep it around, in case of someday finding a car to go with it. And here, between rows of paperback romances, sits the *Consumer Reports Buying Guide* for 1954, a fat, important-looking work, perhaps useful today for appraising the assembled rummage.

I pick up a slim volume in textbook green, *The Ship's Medicine Chest and First Aid at Sea*, printed by the U.S. Public Health Service in 1929, though we're almost as far from the sea here as we are from 1929. I open it and learn that for "Alcoholism (drunkenness)" I should "induce vomiting with several spoonfuls of mustard dissolved in a pint of warm water and then put the patient to bed." I like that. It sounds calm and nonjudgmental, almost motherly: sailors will be sailors. Further, I should not cut off people's arms and legs at sea if I'm less than three days from port and my medicine chest should hold plenty of turpentine, to be used externally for pleurisy, colds, bronchitis, and lumbago.

This is plainly a gold mine, and I dig out my nickel for the volunteer firemen. Waiting in line, I muse on my unknown neighbors who have kept this book handy for sixty-five years, and suddenly remember that this sale is an annual event. Every year, the sale collects from and sells to the same small North Hill population. If, this year, we were finally persuaded to part with the 1954 *Buying Guide* and the 1960 dress patterns, what on earth did we surrender last year? Gentlemen's knee breeches and powdered wigs? Blunderbusses, butter churns, ox yokes, washboilers? Hoopskirts and whalebone corsets; the running board from a Chandler Six? I should have come last year. I've always wanted an ox yoke; I'm sure it would come in handy.

At the end of *their* sale, the fire and rescue needs the space in the fire hall for their trucks and, on Tuesday nights, their bingo game, so they hire a Dumpster for the leavings. Several Dumpsters. And now, at long last, the stuff has become officially trash and takes its much-delayed journey to its permanent home.

City folk, disposing of stuff so effortlessly, live with the carefree feeling that once they've thrown it away, it's *gone*. It isn't. Stuff is eternal. Stuff is, overwhelmingly, nonbiodegradable. Like nuclear waste, stuff has a half-life of roughly forever, give or take a year. And it keeps coming.

I buy new things reluctantly now. If the old things get rickety or make a funny noise, I keep on using them until they belch blue smoke and sparks. Then I wedge them into the basement with the empty paint cans to wait for the fire and rescue squad.

· · · · · ·

Collectors' Items 133

a dish to share

. . . .

Having dropped off my car at the gas station for its oil change, I settle into the diner — called Diner — next door to fill the wait with lunch. It's Thursday, and just as surely as Monday means stuffed pork chops, winter or summer, good times or bad, Thursday means meat loaf, mashed potatoes with gravy, lima beans, roll and butter, iced tea or coffee. The price is $3.90. The lunch special is always $3.90. Most customers order it automatically, though there's always pork barbecue with coleslaw as an alternate. Life here may not be exciting but it's reliable.

Far to the east a luncher can order tofu, or pita with bean sprouts in it, or pop into a restaurant that serves nothing but flavored coffees. Bean sprouts have been around for decades, but they haven't seeped out this way yet and I can't see them coming. Somewhere on the other side of the county seat there's a bean sprouts barrier, and it feels permanent. Coffee here comes only in regular or decaf.

At the next table a wiry young man with remarkable biceps

calls after the waitress, "Make that double potatoes. And extra gravy." She beams over her shoulder at him like a proud mother, happy for his appetite.

Around here, a hearty appetite is still a virtue.

Virtue is simpler here. In civilized places, virtue is an all-day job and gets more complicated every year. City folk need to count the number of fruits and vegetables they've eaten today and remember not to call Indians "Indians" or the waitress "hon." (Here, we call her Fran.) They need to measure the miles they've run, buy only what can be recycled, distinguish between good and bad cholesterol, and keep track of how to feel about Serbs and the homeless. The possibilities for sin keep multiplying and the rules keep changing, which makes city folk anxious and grouchy.

Hereabouts, it's easier. Most of it was settled ages ago, a ten-step program carved in stone, and as long as we aren't killing or coveting or sacrificing a sheep to heathen idols, as long as we raise our kids up right and give our neighbor a hand when he needs it, we can pretty much leave our virtue alone and get on about our business.

The waitress lays my lunch before me and moves the catsup bottle within easy reach. "Anything else?" she asks cheerily.

Else? Massive slabs of meat loaf tilt over the plate's edge, elbowed by half a pound of limas and a sofa cushion of mashed potatoes, and over all oozes a lava of richly brown and aromatic homemade gravy. At other tables men and women alike are lighting into their specials with no sign of dismay; the wiry young man has been served his double potatoes in a soup bowl. Not to be outdone, I take fork in hand.

Having once been city folk, I enjoy a passing twinge of

. . . . . .

A Dish to Share 135

guilt, but the awful truth is that between this great motherly plateful of food and a bean sprout, there's simply no contest.

If the virtue police are right, this should be a ghost county by now. The simplest standard breakfast at this diner should have killed us all. And there's an ashtray on every table, many of them in use; Virginia owes her very existence to tobacco and hasn't defected. And on Friday nights beer is drunk, and the beer drinker, having no choice, drives home; he knows this is dangerous, but he feels no more sinful than he feels when driving without a seat belt, which he also does.

I have yet to pass a jogger on the roads, but sometimes, driving toward the civilized east, I slam on the brakes for a weekend bike rider. As I edge around him on a blind curve, praying not to meet an oncoming pickup truck, I can see by his face that bike riding is a virtue where he comes from. He's even wearing special clothes for it, ludicrous and indecent by local standards, so all can see that this is no casual jaunt but a noble endeavor. From my point of view he's more dangerous than the beer drinker and harder to avoid, since I can stay off the roads after midnight on Fridays, but who can compete with virtue?

The waitress reappears, and I notice with a slight shock that I've absentmindedly eaten everything she brought me except the catsup bottle. "The pie today is lemon chiffon," she says, clearly expecting me to take advantage of the offer; the man with the double potatoes is eating *his* lemon chiffon. He looks every bit as virtuous as the bike rider, but happier.

The general rule seems to be that if it wasn't a sin forty years ago, or a thousand years ago, it probably isn't a sin today.

I realize that this is all very wrong and backward of us, and we shall surely perish from our accumulated wickedness, but it certainly does make life easier.

The garageman sticks his head through the door and signals that my car is ready. I pay my $3.90 at the register — nobody here brings you a check; you just tell them what you've eaten — and stagger out into the sunshine, happily replete with sin and gravy.

"Is THAT ALL you're going to take? That's Susan's, you know. She always makes that, and it's just delicious. Here, you'd better have some more."

I smile weakly down at my loaded plate. This isn't dinner, or even lunch, merely a meeting of the fair-planning committee, but ritual offerings have been brought and must be eaten. Eating attends all our public functions.

Civilized people eat at home or in restaurants or at dinner parties. Here we eat in public, at trestle tables in the fire hall, the 4-H barn, the church fellowship hall, the chairperson's living room, elbow to elbow with neighbors. After the event there's a genteel scramble to reclaim the pots and bowls. Phone calls go around: a Pyrex pie plate and a flowered platter have been left behind; does anyone know their owners?

No school function or fund-raising event is complete without its bake sale, and the smell of brownies hovers over every village. No religious occasion, however solemn, passes unmarked by a potluck supper, the covered dishes borne reverently across the parking lot and into the church like sacrifices.

The offerings are made by hand. It would be unthinkable to buy potato salad at the deli counter and pass it off as one's own, and I'm sure nobody ever does. For the family, yes, and to judge from the grocery carts frozen pizza and boxed macaroni-and-cheese are as popular here as anywhere. Food offered in public, though, must make a statement, serve as a signature tune. Plagiarism would be a crime against selfhood.

The offering can be the same for every event, sometimes for generations of the same family, marking one's lineage and personal identity. It is, say, Alice Powell who makes those bite-sized mince pies. The pies *are* Alice; for another woman to bring bite-sized mince pies would be a shocking trespass. She would be usurping Alice's place in the world's eye. Pretending to *be* Alice. Stealing her face.

Often there's a distinctive stamp to the recipe, unique to the family and a secret, though rumor may have it that Helen, like her mother and grandmother, puts a cup of mayonnaise in the sauce, or a spoonful of lime Jell-O in the Easter cake. An unbridgeable gulf, however, divides distinctive from pretentious. As long as Helen sticks to the local supermarket she can't go wrong, but if she drove to the sophisticated east and came back with sun-dried tomatoes, goat's cheese, and cilantro, she would slip beyond the pale and into social oblivion. She doesn't, though. Tradition is sacred here. Alien food would be a kind of culinary flag-burning.

Early in my own rural life I brought an offering to a community function. Memory draws a merciful veil over its exact nature, but I think it contained tabbouleh with fresh mint leaves. At evening's end, with all eyes upon me, I covered it up and hurried it back to my car. All of it. Every spoonful. Not only the Amish can shun.

When meat is involved, men as well as women take part in the ritual feasts. No man may make a salad or bake a cake, but where there's meat, there are men, and a man may win fame for his turkey stuffing or his inimitable touch with barbecue. (Barbecue here, as everywhere, is a male preserve, and it would be as outrageous a taboo violation for women to approach a barbecue pit as for them to kill and dress their own venison.)

Barbecue is a staple at fund-raisers. When money is charged for food, instead of individual offerings the menu features a single, traditional item, year after year. Often, money *is* charged. In civilized places the government or someone pays for everything, but out here beyond the sidewalks, if we want a playground or a new fire truck we throw a fund-raiser. Fund-raisers include raffles, rummage sales, entertainment for the children, and food. Always food. Annual pancake breakfasts. Annual barbecues. Monthly ham-and-turkey dinners. Ice-cream socials, with volunteers needed to turn the cranks. Spaghetti dinners. (Nobody who called spaghetti "pasta" would be planning to attend anyway.) Men cook in a group, in full view, because men get lonesome alone in a kitchen. Every fall, men supervise the cider press and tend and stir the cauldron of apple butter. Women serve, pour iced tea, and clean up afterward.

The public lines up with plates. The plates are filled. The new American fear of food has yet to find its way down our lanes, and everyone smiles and jostles along the rows of benches and squeezes between neighbors balancing toppling mounds of pancakes and sausage, or barbecue and coleslaw, or turkey and gravy.

Everyone eats. Watching, the philosophical might reflect on the prevalence of community feasting in ancient history, in the Bible, and in folk and fairy tales, and how perhaps its gravies formed the glue of common purpose and the lubricant

· · · · · ·

of civic peace, but we aren't philosophers here. We just eat, praising the food in detail between mouthfuls, and pass the baskets of potato chips back and forth among our neighbors.

FOOD APPEARS even in the relatively sophisticated precincts of the editorial offices. The round table that's supposed to hold rival newspapers for reference always holds, on top of them, paper plates of homemade fudge or carrot cake; boxes of tomatoes, peaches, and apples in their seasons; or at the very least the remains of a box of jelly doughnuts. For approaching births or weddings, even the cops-and-courts reporter brings food, and the bounty spreads from the round table to the neighboring desks and shelves: potato salad, coleslaw, four kinds of sliced cheese, sliced ham, sliced roast beef, sliced turkey, gargantuan pickles, rolls, three kinds of bread, potato chips, cheese dips, crackers, homemade oatmeal cookies, homemade poppy-seed cake, a store-bought sheet cake commemorating the occasion, Coke, Diet Coke, iced tea. We eat ourselves sick like ancient Romans and go glassy-eyed back to our computer terminals.

I SUPPOSE food is still celebrated here because food was once the central fact of life. It was what the land did for a living; it was all things to all people here.

Twenty years ago I could stand on the deck of this house and look across the valley and food was everywhere. Potential milk and cheese, bread and butter, steak and eggs, corn muffins, lamb chops, applesauce, and peach cobbler were laid on the table of the valley within easy walking distance of my house in case all the trucks in the country should run out of gas. Wherever you went in the valley — and even here on the mountain where the air currents flick sound upward along with the hawks — cows and roosters were the white noise, unregistered but always resident in the ear.

There was something reassuring about seeing and hearing the meals of the future; something secure about living next door to them, rather than trying to imagine the valley on the far side of the continent where, I'm told, underpaid migrants now grow more than half the fruits and vegetables we eat, in soil fast salting up from irrigation. Some 85 percent, they say, of the West's water goes for irrigation. Isn't there something perverse about growing our food on land that has to be forced to grow it, in a climate that flatly rejects it? And what will happen when the water dries up, or the soil sours, or California cracks loose and floats away into the Pacific? Can we plow our subdivisions back into our own rich dirt and replant it? Eat the dandelions out of all the new lawns?

We're told not to worry. It's all being taken care of for us, and the food of the future will be grown in chemically treated, recirculated water under artificial suns. We will feed the world from a patch of ground no bigger than a football field. No bigger than a coffee table.

In my valley, in the 1950s, there were three hundred dairy herds, but the price of milk has stagnated for fifteen years and now we're down to three herds and counting.

Never mind, soon all the country's milk will come from half-a-dozen chemically treated cows.

I realize America's future lies in information management, not food, and some technological types I know actually believe food is produced by their telephones, in the form of pizza or restaurant reservations. Still, I miss looking at food in a field. I rejoice at the occasional hand-lettered sign in the

· · · · · ·

A Dish to Share 141

supermarket offering lambs butchered to order, and surely, in the meat case, those quivering, gelatinous hog maws and tidy little bunches of pigs' feet, even packets of triangular pigs' ears, perhaps for making silk purses, must come from local creatures still raised in some cranny of the valley. For how much longer now? Hogs and new half-million-dollar houses are natural enemies.

With binoculars I can see where the peach orchard was. Half of the hillside is now enormous new houses and half of it's golf course, because you can't sell a really expensive house these days unless there's a golf course attached. All summer when I drive by, its water sprinklers are cycling endlessly, next to this town that has always had summer water shortages. In August the grass is an eye-stinging green between the parched fields.

Following the rule that developments must be named for whatever it was they replaced — Rolling Meadows, Forest Glen — it's called The Orchard. Of course people do need to play golf, but what shall we do for peaches?

high noon

· · · · · · · · · · · · · · · ·

North Hill isn't really my closest village, only the closest useful village. My mail is addressed to Pikestown. If the trees were cleared, I could roll straight down the mountain to its only street.

Pikestown actually was a town a hundred years ago and took in summer boarders who rode the train — there actually was a train a hundred years ago — out from the muggy city to sit on porches and breathe our air and carry picnics up the mountain. Before that, before the Civil War, it was already a place of real substance, with four carpenters, five shoemakers, two stores, two taverns, three tailors, three blacksmiths, two saddlers, a tannery, several doctors, a church, a school, and a post office.

After World War II, after the train stopped, it dwindled steadily until it could no longer be considered a town, barely even a village. It's hard to imagine a doctor's office within ten miles now, and four years ago even the post office closed.

We used the one in North Hill five miles away. Postal box

holders there had to squeeze in together to make room for the villagers' temporary boxes, though they were gracious about it, as if welcoming refugees in from a flood. We were allowed to keep our zip code, our last scrap of dignity, but it lived in someone else's house.

We'd had a post office since 1806, and losing it came as a shock. Nobody seemed to know why the postal service closed us down so suddenly. The rumor was that an inspector had found it unsafe, our honest little two-room wooden building. It was hard to imagine what threats it concealed; if the whole structure had fallen on the head of a postal patron it would scarcely have raised a lump. Cynics felt this was merely an excuse. We were considered too small to bother with, not worth the mail truck's trouble. Appeals were lodged. Letters were written to congressmen. Petitions were signed. Hopes were raised and then dashed again. Time passed.

The village, already marginal, languished. To be a village at all and not just a string of houses along a country road, a place needs a minimum of a post office and a general store, functions that, in some places, are still under the same roof and interdependent. In our village the post office was down the road from the store, but when the post office closed the store staggered. Outlying people like me had no reason to turn off the highway and wind down the switchbacks to pick up a loaf of bread and a newspaper at the store. We drove our packages to the North Hill post office and stopped at the North Hill general store, which was bigger and better anyway, carried perishables like milk and eggs, and almost always got its supply of newspapers, though occasional unwary shoppers like me came home with yesterday's.

Our own general store starved to death, leaving the village

. . . . . .

to drift in limbo with no public place at all. Then an adventurous villager bought it and repainted its sign and struggled to keep going on sales of soda and candy to infrequent hikers and the handful of village children. Most of the time he sat behind the counter reading paperbacks.

The wheels ground slowly, but they did grind. Somewhat to everyone's surprise, half a field in the village was purchased, and the new post office slowly began to rise, bland but sturdy. Catty-corner across the road from it, at the old post office, the porch steps sagged and the roof grew moss. The new one triumphantly facing it was made of brick, setting it apart as official, because around here barns and small houses are built of wood and big houses are built of stone, and brick is only for official places, from the stately court-house in the county seat to the remotest volunteer fire department. Being the only official building for miles around, our new post office couldn't look stranger here if it had been mad King Ludwig's castle, but militant villagers had at least held out for our traditional red standing-seam metal roof instead of government-issue shingles.

It was finished, and rumored to be opening soon. It was inspected for safety and passed muster. The village hovered. Finally one day the North Hill postmistress told me, though not inhospitably, that Pikestown was once again properly sanctioned to communicate with the world. She said she would miss us all terribly.

I passed through the village late that night and swerved in alarm. The new post office lights up at night. It lights up violently, in an unnatural shade of white, maybe like cancer cells illuminated by some fancy diagnostic process. How can the village sleep? You'd think they'd all converge on it

. . . . . .

howling at three in the morning and throw a blanket over it, like covering the cage of a squawking parrot. The village won in the matter of the county's new lights at the community center by simply not turning them on, but I suppose the national Postal Service doesn't take insubordination from country villages. I suppose, like surveillance cameras in the chain stores, blinding post offices have been mandated by those who know more about crime than we do.

ON A HOT BUGGY MORNING I go down to the village to celebrate.

By day, for the dedication ceremony, it's a harmless little building around which fifty or sixty villagers, maybe the entire in-town population, have gathered on folding chairs, fanning gnats with their programs. I don't see any of my mountain neighbors; mountain folk and village folk rarely mix. The only faces I recognize are our congressman and our state senator, both up for reelection.

The postmistress, resuming her interrupted reign, stands on the concrete apron that serves as a porch and makes some grateful introductory remarks. Behind her a red, white, and blue plastic ribbon ties the little pillars together, waiting to be cut.

She introduces the minister. As he rises to give the invocation, we bow our heads and a fellow in back of us fires up a large mowing machine and begins to mow the other half of the field. The minister shouts gamely over the racket. He blesses the United States Postal Service at considerable length for not abandoning us. He blesses our postal district manager, on hand for the occasion, and those who collect and sort the mail and those who deliver it. He blesses us, the postal patrons who send and receive, and most particularly the new building in which we shall do so. Amen.

At the "amen" the mowing machine concludes its labors and drives away through a gap in the hedgerow.

Two local Cub Scouts raise a specially donated flag that has flown over the United States Capitol for an unstated period of time. It hangs crooked; the scouts have fastened it wrong. We rise and salute it, our concerted mumble hovering like gray wool in the heavy air.

The president of the citizens association takes over the concrete porch and hands out framed certificates of thanks to all who have worked so hard toward this glorious day. Each certificate is received with a few polite and modest words. Then she turns the proceedings over to our congressman, a neat little man with the hopeless energy of a master of ceremonies at a run-down resort hotel. He tells a funny story about how he met his future wife. He talks of his interest in the Civil War, and offers us sidelights on its local impact. He doesn't mention the post office. He talks and talks, and we sit patiently on our folding chairs fanning. Finally something — perhaps his wife has a secret signal — silences him, and he gives way to the postal district manager, who will cut the ribbon. We gather around.

Someone hands him the scissors, joke scissors three feet long, designed to be photographed by the media. The ribbon refuses to yield until half-a-dozen people have tried, but finally we troop politely in to look around.

The brightness inside, flooding from panels in walls and ceiling, dwarfs the outside sun. Everything is new; not a single worn familiar counter or brass-trimmed postal box has been pressed back into service. The vinyl-tile flooring glitters. I

· · · · · ·

suppose we really will be able to pick up tearstained love letters here, smudgy postcards from summer camps, tattered packages with handmade sweaters in them, but somehow it seems to promise only insurance forms and tax notices.

For all its glitter, I see by the sign that it will still be closed from twelve to one every day. Food at regular intervals is still a basic human right here.

For the occasion, the citizens association has laid out tables of coffee, homemade muffins, cookies, brownies, eclairs, cream buns, and jugs of the indispensable iced tea. Everyone mills around eating and snapping pictures of the shiny shelves and textured plastic receptacles.

I scald my mouth on coffee and leave. Across the road the weeds have grown up to the windowsills of the old post office and the yellow paint is peeling from its friendly old boards. I suppose no one will ever bother to tear it down.

Never mind; once again our zip code has its own roof over its head. The general store will rise again. The village, by a whisker, survives and wobbles into its third century, remaining a kind of shadow family one remove beyond family, the extra, slightly wider net of concern to break a person's possible fall, or in the last analysis, those who will feed us in time of famine and those we're obliged to feed. Amen.

EVER MINDFUL OF WINTER, I devote a lot of time to appreciating summer, trying to soak up enough to last for a while. Summer on the mountain unfolds slowly, always a few paces behind summer in the valley. Dogwood and daffodils bloom, the feisty, hot-tempered hummingbirds arrive to chase each other away from the feeder, azaleas bloom, then day-lilies, then the purple coneflowers bobbing under the weight of goldfinches and swallowtails. The cats lie flat on the shady deck as if ironed.

In the valley, gardens come into their August glory. This has nothing to do with flowers. Around here the word "garden" means food; flowers are called "flowers," and if someone in the family wants to stick in a marigold here and there, that's fine, but she needn't think she can waste the best dirt, the best sun, on purely cosmetic plants. A real garden is for eating.

End of May, early June, men in the diner ask each other, "Got your garden in yet?" They plant late here, being wary of spring frosts and floods, and they tend to plant all at once. They "get the garden in." Traditionally this is done on Memorial Day weekend, but traditionally it rains floods on Memorial Day weekend and the ground takes another week to dry out to plantability. Whatever the forecast, though, they don't rush the season. Their forebears planted on Memorial Day. Tradition rules.

Hobby gardeners, the folks who have come from away with dreams of wholesome, organically grown vegetables eaten fresh from the good earth, fuss all spring. They plant a row at a time, depending on hardiness, and then listen to the weather bulletins and rush out in the dark with protective pots and caps and plastic tunnels against the coming frost.

Farm people wait. Memorial Day is too late for cool-weather crops like lettuce and spinach, but those salady things are a nuisance anyway. They have no staying power, no sustaining calories, and worse, they have to be eaten at once. There's something childish and undisciplined about eating food right out of the garden, on the same day, instead of saving it up for the needy months of winter.

$\cdots\cdots$

Hobby gardeners brood over their dirt and tinker with its needs as if it were an ailing baby. They send soil samples to the Extension Service to get its pH factor checked, and correct it with lime, and dig in the compost they have laboriously created from kitchen scraps in a special patented bin.

The farmers' sons for the most part work a garden that's been garden for generations. The rocks that called for a crowbar have already been hoisted out, possibly by the gardener's grandfather. Composting potato peelings — their grandmothers fed them to the pigs — seems sissy, a city-folk notion. Real men, even if they don't keep livestock, know where to get a couple of loads of manure. Honest manure, barn muck, rich and drippy and smelling authentically of a winter's worth of urine, strong enough to make your eyes water even driving by on the road. They spread it on the garden and till it under and then go about their business while it sinks in, waiting for Memorial Day.

In spring the general store and even the supermarket stock bins of onion sets. At the hardware store, serious seeds like beans and corn are sold by the pound, scooped up with a ladle and weighed. Onions, beans, corn, tomatoes, beets, squash, cabbages are the essentials of winter survival. Sometimes a prosperous man with space to spare for temporary treats plants melons, but mostly it's crops to keep.

It's a man's work, the badge of responsible male adulthood, this planting. A grown man provides food to winter his family, and even a widower will put in a garden and carry the surplus around to his neighbors, because what kind of useless bum would let the summer go frittering by without corn to be hoed?

· · · · · ·

In July the women take over, and for the next three months they pick and freeze and can and preserve what the garden grew. Even with air-conditioning their kitchens swelter, their faces turn scarlet, and their hair straggles damply. Neighbors help neighbors. My dental hygienist, chipping away at plaque, reports that her mother and sister both live nearby, and over the weekend the three of them got together and put up several dozen quarts of beans. They had a ball, she says, laughing and joking all afternoon.

Nobody needs to do this. Here as everywhere, supermarkets stand ready to feed the family in February. While one's own fresh beans and tomatoes, eaten on the same day, do taste better than the supermarket's, it's doubtful whether we could tell the difference by Christmas, and a canned bean is a canned bean.

Subtler needs are served. Psychologists keep urging us to feel good about ourselves, to cultivate our self-esteem, to remind ourselves in the mirror daily that we are good people, worthy people. Down in the valley, they do it with gardens. The man who has put in his garden and the woman who has canned and frozen and pickled it know they are worthy people. They have done what their forebears did and, supermarket or no supermarket, provisioned their homes.

When they look in the mirror, they feel just fine.

EVERYWHERE IN THE VALLEY towns and villages, summer calls for parades. Sometimes for a special occasion like the Fourth of July, or Heritage Day, or Court Days, and sometimes just because they've always had a parade with decorated bikes and trucks, floats on hay wagons, antique cars, the local fire equipment, the Boy Scouts. And from Memorial Day till snowfall, there are festivals and fairs.

I PAY FOR MY pink ticket and drive lumbering across the dusty field to park between a pickup and a horse van. A good crowd. This is the annual county 4-H fair and serious-looking people come to it, a serious fair without cotton candy or Ferris wheels, because it's about farming and here, at least for the time being, farming is still serious stuff. Here, for a week every year, we can dream that the American family farm lives on; not Nebraska-sized fields tended by brontosaurean machinery, but a woman in an apron carrying a bucket of potato peels to the pigs and coming back with warm fresh eggs. We can believe because a new generation of children is here with their farming products and their blind faith in the future of pigs.

I pay a duty call to the exhibits building, though paper plates of tomatoes and peppers lack drama, the cakes and brownies have been nibbled by judges, and the flower arrangements, now in their fourth day, sag in the heat. After a quick pass through some earnest displays on water conservation, I head outside to the livestock buildings.

Rabbits looking anxious, llamas looking like movie starlets, fancy poultry looking like ladies' hats. A loose duckling. Pens full of pigs. Between two barns there's a hose outlet on a cement slab and children wait in line, each with a sheep on a leash and a bottle of shampoo.

In the judging barn I find a seat in the bleachers in time for the sheep obstacle course. Each child leads forth his sheep and navigates a course over bales of hay. Since hay jumping isn't a sheeply concept, the child keeps lifting his sheep up and setting him (or her) down on the other side. The purpose eludes me, except that the emphasis here is on livestock handling. Not just pouring in the right food and chemicals, but the face-to-face relationship of child and creature, which may involve heavy lifting.

After the heifer obedience class I drift over to the beef building.

In the first stall lies a red Hereford steer the size and shape of a mobile home, and beside him in the clean straw lies a sweet-faced girl of ten or eleven, her head on his shoulder and her arm around his neck. I stop to congratulate her on the blue ribbon in his halter. "What's his name?"

"Handsome," she says shyly. "His name's Handsome."

"And you raised him from a baby?"

She nods proudly. "He's going to get a real good price at the auction tomorrow night, too." She smooths the curls between his big, bland eyes. "Aren't you, Handsome?"

Blue ribbons are all very well, but it's the auction, the price per pound from Giant Foods or Safeway, that's the fair's final report card. The sweet-faced child suddenly seems to me a cold-blooded monster, heartless and greedy. She knows full well the highest bidder for Handsome isn't buying him to keep the grass trimmed. So much for the gentle dream of the family farm, I think bitterly: a little girl sells her pet for meat and doesn't even *mind*. Glad she's not *my* daughter.

In my city days, I'd told myself that it was all right to eat farm animals because we'd fed and vetted and protected them, while wild animals had earned their own living and didn't owe us a nickel, much less their lives. Besides, city folk needn't think of restaurant or supermarket meat as having been *killed*, exactly, not the way a hunter kills a deer. Euthanasia, maybe. Old age.

Perhaps, though, dependent or not, Handsome's life is as valuable to him as a deer's is to a deer. Perhaps if Handsome had Bambi's press agent, McDonald's would go broke.

On the way home I remember there's nothing for dinner and stop at the Safeway. We're beef eaters hereabouts and the steaks and roasts stretch in a red river along the aisle. Just for the moment they look peculiarly mortal, more like roadkills than groceries. *My* roadkills. (Who killed Cock Robin? "I," said the sparrow, "With my bow and arrow.")

I push the cart faster. *Macaroni and cheese*, I think. *Pasta with tomato sauce.*

The next day, though, Handsome's brief life has shifted perspective and I can see him, not at the butcher's, but in a sunny field, knee-deep in sweet grass, waiting for a little girl to come running home from the school bus and rub him between the ears.

A steer is not a household pet, and if no one ate hamburgers then Handsome would never have lived at all, to spend such a pleasant summer in such a green field. Joy is not measured in years, and the steer in the summer's field lives unshadowed by thoughts of the winter's steaks. Surely, if asked, he'd rather have had one sunny summer than no summer at all.

AFTER THE FAIR, people in the suburban eastern half of the county write indignant letters to the newspaper: Their children are being excluded. The 4-H clubs and fairs are not arranged for them. Certainly their daughters don't want to learn to pickle beets and piece quilts or their sons to raise lambs — whatever would be the use? And the citizens' associations that control the eastern world have zoning laws against everything else in 4-H, even growing vegetables. Something will have to be done to include the children of the east and keep them amused at the fair.

The eastern spokespersons have just succeeded in canceling our annual rodeo on the grounds of cruelty and they're drunk with power. The following year the fair, now in its sixtieth year, makes changes, "in line with the county's changing population," as the newspaper puts it. A country dance with live music will be included, pony rides and a nature walk, a "youth talent search."

A skewed and slightly schizophrenic fair sidles toward the future. On one of the barns the old wooden sign saying "Breeding Sheep" has been hastily painted over and a paper sign by the doorway says "Children's Activities." It lists the times for a magic show, "making hats and other fun things with newspaper," "making yarn dolls and button yo-yos," an origami class, and a storyteller. At the moment nothing is happening except several towheaded children chasing each other aimlessly in and out of the empty stalls.

The sheep that once had a whole barn of their own now fit easily into the Swine Barn, across the aisle from the sleeping pigs.

I retreat to the judging barn, where perhaps next year button yo-yos and origami will be assessed, but for now nothing has changed except that some of the classes seem smaller than last year's. The Hereford class has only one entry.

Market Steers are on the line and all entries have been rated "choice." Children of all sizes, many of them barly up to the chins of their charges, lead them in, circle them, line them up. Each child carries an aluminum pole with a bend at the end like a fireplace poker, to prod the steer's legs into place at their most becoming angle and then to slowly, hypnotically, massage the great belly into docility.

As always at a 4-H fair, the judge acts as instructor, explaining and describing each animal. The word "meat" is often on his lips, and he speaks it lovingly, almost longingly. Fat is bad, bone is bad, meat is good. "A lot of red meat there," he says, and "a walking meat market," and "packed full of red meat." He speaks of "muscle expression," "better profiling," and "a cleaner package," which calls up visions of the supermarket's Styrofoam tray and plastic wrap, but he means the way the creature is put together, its length of back and leg and breadth of rib. One, he says, "will probably kill a little better than you might think," and I study the girl's face for a wince, but she looks pleased.

For some reason the girls outnumber the boys by almost four to one; will the women here be the last holdouts, digging their toes in on their farms, manning their tractors under the Palladian windows of the new suburbs? When we get down to the championship there are seven girls and only two boys. Slowly they parade the three-quarter-ton beasts around the ring. For the most part the creatures follow trustingly, but once in a while they balk and stare around with huge, baffled eyes as if suspicion had flickered across their gentle brains; some foretaste of their mission in life. Little girls of eight or nine brace their feet in the sawdust and tug valiantly at leashes.

Behind me in the bleachers, a man has brought his family from the suburbs. He keeps urging his son to look at the nice cows; the boy squirms and gouges my back with his knees and says he wants to go see horsies.

The judge announces the champion, the reserve champion, and the runners-up by slapping their rumps in order; they shy nervously and are led away through the big doors into the blazing sun.

I follow them. Outside, in an improvised rope ring, a man in a cowboy hat is giving pony rides, leading the littlest kids around in a dusty circle on comatose piebald Shetlands. The children clutch the saddle horn and stare straight ahead, patiently enduring.

For the first time there's a cotton-candy stand.

The following year there are carnival rides and booths selling everything from cosmetics to satellite dishes, and 4-H has withdrawn its official support.

I go west across the mountain instead, to the weeklong fair in the next county over where they still have a greased-pig scramble with a real pig.

DIRECTLY BELOW MY DECK lie the 420 acres where cows used to thread their way along their accustomed paths to the barn to be milked, followed by their long afternoon shadows. The dairy farmer and his wife have four sons and a daughter, but none of them wanted to farm. Shortly after I moved here, he began to search for someone to buy his place and work it. After four years he gave up, divided it into parcels, and sold it for building lots.

His house has stood on its land since 1787. Up until yesterday the village gathered there for celebrations. It's been bought by a catering service. Sometimes city couples come out to be married in a tent on its lawn. I don't know what

· · · · · ·

will become of the catering; it seems an odd business to start up in a world where people split their own stovewood, but no doubt the owners have an eye on the future.

Three new houses have been built there so far, looking accidental in the expanse of pasture. They're set at an odd angle to the road. All the new houses springing up here in the west are slightly skewed, though I suppose it's harder to figure out where to put a house in a field than beside a road. Clumps of new houses all sit catty-corner, their shoulders turned to each other, as if dropped rather than built. Perhaps on paper the effect was charmingly casual, but in practice it just looks messy and rather temporary, houses come from away and still in transit.

I can't tell whether people have moved into the dairy-farm houses yet, to carry on their lives under my disapproving eye. That's the thing about the new people. They hide their cars in garages, they don't plant gardens or keep livestock or send up chimney smoke from woodstoves, and their children don't play outdoors, so you can't tell whether they're there at all.

I suppose it's nothing to cry about. My whole generation has seen its childhood landscapes changed, and America loses a million acres of farmland a year and thinks nothing of it. But this county was first in the area in milk production. The glittering aluminum trucks roved the roads collecting ten-gallon cans of milk from the ends of lanes. We weren't just famous for quantity, either; the quality of our milk was praised by the cognoscenti and for a long time most of our herds were pure Guernsey, their milk rich enough to coat a spoon. After everyone switched to the megaproducing black-and-white holsteins, each family still kept a Guernsey among

· · · · · ·

them, a dainty little blond with poetic dark eyes, for their own personal butter and cream.

Now, regular as clockwork, the newspaper sends a photographer and a reporter out to interview another county farmer closing down.

Henry Stowers, the third generation on his two-hundred-acre farm near the new toll road, told the reporter he only kept on farming so the land would look pretty to a developer whenever he happened by. Within a couple of weeks, as if charmed into appearing, a developer happened by and bought it. It was briefly mentioned in the paper, but nobody said where Henry Stowers went.

Sam Welsh, seventh generation, has just closed his Green Hill dairy farm. He blames his troubles on urbanization and the subsequent tangle of property rights and taxes. The new people, needing new schools and civilized services, resent the lower agricultural taxes; they want more money from farmers.

The Browns are leaving the East entirely. Bob Brown is a sixth-generation farmer whose family settled here in 1757, and this week he's shipping his cattle to their new place in Oklahoma and leaving three thousand of the richest acres in Virginia, where houses will grow next year.

The Browns are angry. They're particularly angry at the preservationists and agricultural agents who urge our farmers to solve their problems creatively, to move with the times, to switch to boutique products like Christmas trees, cut flowers, flower seeds, and organic strawberries to truck into Washington and sell at specialty markets. Goat cheese is recommended, and llamas, emus, and pick-your-own orchards. The farmers' wives can turn the farmhouses into bed-and-breakfasts, with hayrides and a petting zoo.

. . . . . .

Farmers who have grown serious, useful food are insulted when told to grow shiitake mushrooms for the city's restaurants. It's undignified. And unlikely to support a family, or even pay the new taxes.

In the last five years, some twenty western farmers have taken up what they call "entertainment farming." Families from the sanitary suburbs drive out and pay money to marvel at the sight of real dirt with real food on it. "An agricultural amusement park," one farmer calls it. Trail rides and campfires are offered, and a chance to play at rounding up the steers. One farm has become a sort of countrified country club where, for $645 a year, a family of suburbanites can come and pick flowers and vegetables, fish in the pond, ride a horse.

An idealistic couple, inspired by magazine articles, tried to sell shares of their Brookfarm production. For payment in advance, subscribers got a thirty-quart cooler of fresh-picked organic vegetables every week for three months. It was a disaster. Customers couldn't understand why the tomatoes weren't ready till July or the corn till August, why they couldn't have asparagus all summer, and why the harvest included so many things their children wouldn't eat. The operation folded after a single season.

The Browns' new neighbors in the new houses complained constantly about the smells and sounds of farm life. Their teenagers drove cars across the fields. Grain markets and the shops that mend agricultural equipment have retreated a long drive west beyond the mountains. Banks that had been established to serve farmers now eyed them skeptically.

Just before they leave, Mrs. Brown writes a farewell letter

to the newspaper, concluding, "Will the last real farmer to leave the county please remember to shut the gate?"

One man of long memory counters with a letter saying that farming in the county was by no means dead, just undergoing one of its periodic downturns, and did nobody remember the Great Drought of 1930? Did nobody remember the hog cholera?

But back then only the farmers were lost. Other farmers took over their fields. This time the fields themselves will be lost, and there aren't any other fields.

Thoreau said he was making the earth say beans instead of grass. We make it say houses instead of beans. Perhaps the county could pass a law that all new houses must be built out of gingerbread and candied cherries, like the witch's house in "Hansel and Gretel." Then, in a pinch, we could eat them.

worlds apart

·················

I acquired another cat, someone's barn cat out to better himself, a fine, strong tabby with white toes and a commanding voice. He comes home from his rabbit-farming chores shouting up the driveway, "Attention, please! The cat is coming!" Morgan, a sociable cat, likes him, and I feel he is, if not an actual gift from the mountain, at least a token of my acceptance here. I call him General Pickett, mindful that the disastrous charge and slaughter were *not his fault*, and he never forgave Lee for the order that killed his men.

I sell another book, and the wolf retreats his customary two paces from the door. Everyone at the gas station knows my name, though some of them call me "dear" instead. Once a week I have lunch with a friend from the newspaper at a restaurant in a converted chicken shed, out back under the oak tree in summer, huddled around the heater in winter. I have stopped referring to Philadelphia as "back home."

I may not have a circle of friends and family here, but I no longer feel surrounded by strangers. For one thing, they keep smiling at me, wide, generous smiles that at first made me wonder if I was wearing something unusually amusing or had lipstick on my nose.

No alternative way to live has opened before me and I suppose I'll be staying awhile. I may have to. I've lost my grip on the very concept of ill will and am no longer fit for urban living, or even urban visiting. I leave my car unlocked; sometimes I leave the key in the ignition. While staying at friends' apartments I can't make their door keys work or remember the sequence of the locks or the code to disable the burglar alarm. And I speak to strangers.

I spoke to a man on the Washington Metro. He got on at the Dupont Circle Station and chose a seat across from me. Crouching to sit, he paused and stared at the ad on the wall behind him, a picture of a car, with the explanation, "Tear Up Your Metro Card."

He seemed baffled, so I said, "I know, I was wondering about that myself. What do you think it means?"

He snapped his head around. Instantly, automatically, his features clamped into that stony cast common to city folk who have been addressed by strangers. Suspicions flickered visibly through his mind: was I prostitute or panhandler, possible pickpocket, or merely another wandering nutcase?

I think he decided on the last. Perhaps my clothes justified the analysis. I'm never sure what to wear in the city and my urban suits have developed that unloved, thrift-shop sag from life in the back of the closet. All I know about current modes is what I read in magazines, which tell me that properly dressed ladies now wear elastic miniskirts or hot pants and expose their breasts. Surely I would have looked even loonier exposed?

· · · · · ·

The man sat down, forced to face me but keeping his eyes fixed on the wall over my head, lest I should be encouraged to speak again. I wanted to apologize, but that would have made it worse.

In the valley it's considered rude *not* to speak to strangers; to pretend that they don't exist, aren't standing there beside you sniffing melons in the produce department, or to brush them off with the curt, commercial, "Have a nice day." Somehow "Y'all have a good one now, hear?" never seems spoken under orders.

Out here, speaking is as natural as breathing. The young speak to the old, black people to white, and the waitress at the diner to the owner of hundreds of fenced acres dotted with racehorses: "Whatever happened to that rain they promised us?" she asks, setting down his iced tea. He shakes his head. "I don't know. Everything's just burning up. Fields are brown."

The clerk in the hardware store asks a customer if he's sold that old Dodge truck yet, because he might have a buyer for it. The cheerful woman who pumps gas and washes windshields tells me about her trip to Baltimore.

The checkout line at the supermarket is moving slowly. The man at the register doesn't know what to get his wife for her birthday and he's soliciting suggestions. The first woman in line says, "Get her something pretty to wear," but he doesn't know what size. When the next woman's groceries slide up the counter, she says, "Why not flowers?" "Plenty of flowers of our own," he says. "Take her out to dinner, then." The flow of groceries stops while they consider the choice of local restaurants, dominated by McDonald's and Dunkin' Donuts.

. . . . . .

Many of these exchanges aren't actually between strangers at all, much of the population being native here, but the natives graciously don't discriminate between me and their high-school classmates. If my face isn't immediately familiar, why, maybe it should be, or will be next time.

In the city, once a stranger, always a stranger. We know no more about the man in the corner news booth after we've bought our hundredth morning paper than before we bought our first. No information is exchanged; we needn't even ask the paper's price.

Here, information flows like water. It's hard to consider the postmistress a stranger after she's told you by how many percentage points (five) she reduced her mortgage. At the general store, a woman buying milk and dog food shares her indignation with her son's soccer coach. He has favorites; her son almost never gets to play, and he's better than half the boys who play every game. When I see her again — and I will — I'll think of her son, game after game scowling idly on the bench.

Walking down the streets of the city, ascending in crowded elevators, standing in lines, our flesh feels threatened by the press of fellow humans whom we do not know and never will. It's easy to think of them as hostile, and we cut our eyes away from theirs.

On my way back home from the city I stop off at the supermarket. A strange man in the parking lot nods approvingly at me and says, "Handy-looking little car you got there. Bet you can go *anywhere* in that," and gets into his own and drives away.

I GO EAST less and less. All my life I'd lived on the eastern edge of the country and all my inner compasses pointed toward the Atlantic. Now I can feel the heavy pull of the interior of the continent, that great bulk looming between the coastal slices and widely believed to be unpopulated. Flying over it, civilized people pull down the shade and watch the movie. From here, it tugs at my shoulder blades from the other side of the mountain. I can see it from my mailbox up on the road. It begins to feel more familiar than the east.

THE EDITOR IN CHIEF of the newspaper prowls the newsroom, seeking advice. He has to go east. He has an appointment on the far side of Washington and he can't figure out how to get there without setting tire on Beltway.

To the rest of the country the Washington Beltway is a metaphor for bureaucracy; to us, it's cannibal country. The playground of the psycho-killers. The River of No Return. Newsmen are known as a tough and fearless tribe, but Joe the editor is not a happy newsman. "Let's face it," he says, "people get killed on that thing."

The editorial staff puts its collective head together and cobbles up a complicated plan involving a ferry across the Potomac and a web of back roads that will snake him around the Beltway and its demonic Siamese twin, I-95, and — if he doesn't get lost — lead to his appointment. The route roughly parallels that of General Jubal Anderson Early in his sneak attack on the city. It will take Joe all morning, but he beams with satisfaction as he pockets the instructions. "Those people are crazy," he explains.

Down at the tavern, a man who's been forced into a journey on the eastern highways will recount his adventure over and over, like a refugee from the Alamo, and at the close of the tale he always says, "Those people are crazy." His listeners nod and chant the response: "Those people are crazy."

It isn't the quantity or the speed of the cars that strikes terror into the traveler's heart; it's the people inside them. It's the conviction that, should he hesitate for the shadow of a second over which exit to take, his fellow motorists will fall on him howling, rend him to splinters, and drink his blood.

Around here we tend to be patient and peaceable drivers. Most of the men have ample chances to prove their manly strength and skill during the day's work, and this keeps their testosterone from bottling up and choking them. At the main intersection in the county seat, it's not uncommon for a cautious farmer to sit through three cycles of the traffic light before venturing a left turn, while the rest of us pile up behind him and wait. Silently. Here, the sound of a horn means that someone has recognized a friend, who will tap his own horn in acknowledgment.

If a driver cuts around us at breakneck speed, chances are his wife is in the final stage of labor. Most of the time, we're on our way to the lumberyard or the feed and grain and it doesn't much matter when we get there. The county's motto is "I Byde my Tyme." I stopped taking the four-lane bypass to the county seat and use the old road now, the business road through the little towns, so I can see whether the blue house on Main Street has found a buyer and whether the big willow in North Hill went down in the last storm.

To THE EAST, people's journeys are more important and their day's supply of time is never adequate to its demands. Even if it were, the habit of hurry has tightened around them and burrowed into their very flesh.

......

Worlds Apart 167

Besides, they're more competitive than we are. More ambitious. Competition leaked out of our gene pool a hundred years ago, when the ambitious left to play in the major leagues of life. Those remaining don't much care whose car pulls ahead. We don't take it personally. To the east, it's a bitter pill; in the great race for success, the faster traveler is beating the slower, who shall be forever disgraced if he doesn't catch up before Exit 22, and woe to those who impede him. He is angry at being beaten. The sight of cars ahead of him makes him angry. Hurry, whether he needs to hurry or not, makes him angrier. A swirling cloud of anger hangs over the eastern highways and the inlander smells it and shies like a frightened horse.

Luckily our unimportance tends to keep us to the west. The coastal cities rarely need us; our errands are more likely in Shippensburg or Hagerstown or Roanoke than on Capitol Hill. We can take I-81. We feel at home on 81. It's an inland road, traveled by people like us, slanting southwesterly down from New York into Tennessee as if shrinking, like us, from the eastern madness. And all along it travels hand in hand with its elderly little sister, Route 11, so whenever we're hungry or sleepy or tired of trucks we can nip over and dawdle through her towns for a while.

In July, like all sensible people, we yearn for the taste and smell of the Atlantic. The Atlantic is due east. The beaches of Delaware and Maryland call us, but they lie on the far side of dragon country. To safely go east we must first go west, to 81, and follow its inland course down beyond the world of anger and importance. Then we can turn left and swing over to the Carolinas, to Nags Head, Ocracoke, Myrtle Beach. It's a long way around, but worth it.

. . . . . .

Joe the editor returns late to the office. He has spent most of the day in his car; he had to wait for the ferry, and he got lost twice, but he's well pleased.

"Those people are crazy," he says.

"Beyond the Wild Wood comes the Wide World," said the Rat. "And that's something that doesn't matter, either to you or me. I've never been there, and I'm never going, nor you either if you've got any sense at all. Don't ever refer to it again, please. Now, then! Here's our backwater at last, where we're going to lunch."

COASTING DOWN the mountain road I see a car poised in its driveway, waiting for me to go by. There's something sinister about the driver. I tap the brakes and stare, thinking *this man is up to no good*, and study him in the mirror as he pulls in behind me.

He's wearing a suit. That's it. Suit, shirt, tie. I have never seen a suit on the mountain before, and it looks like the garment of dastardly purposes. What's he doing here, dressed like that? A banker or lawyer, come with a notice of foreclosure? Come buzzardlike with news of a death in the family? Out from the city to serve a subpoena? Or maybe, to be charitable, he's on his way to a funeral.

Or, it occurs to me, he could just be one of our usually invisible population, a commuter jolted out of his routine by some crisis. I didn't think there were any on the mountain yet.

We hereabouts know of these people in theory, but we never see them. They pass by in the dark, like possums, streaming eastward before dawn while we're sleeping, then back again while we're eating dinner. They have important

· · · · · ·

jobs in the cities to the east, jobs in marketing communications, facilitation strategy, systems analysis, and developmental implementation, while the natives here mostly just build things or grow things or fix things, dress in useful clothes, wash themselves after work instead of before, and arrange their errands westward.

We don't see commuters on weekends, either. They don't loiter over bolts and hasps in the hardware store or coffee in the diner. I think they must get back in their cars and head east again toward the malls where they feel at home. They don't turn out for the softball games in Firemen's Field; they aren't seen digging in gardens; they don't play bingo. They don't come to the Friday dances or volunteer at the hospital. They're invisible.

At least, for the time being, they're invisible here in the countrified western half of the county. In the east, closer to their important jobs, they've risen up and multiplied and taken over the landscape. In one village over there, the mailman by ancient tradition made 243 mail stops a day; now, in less than ten years, the mailing addresses have ballooned to 7,000. What used to be the village is gone and the natives have vanished. I don't know what happened to them, any more than I know what happened to the Indians. Maybe some of them intermarried with the new people, put on suits, and got important jobs. Probably most of them took the money from their cornfields and pastures and emigrated west, over the mountains, out of the county, where taxes are lower and a person can still buy parts for a threshing machine.

Once in a while there'll be a human-interest story in the city newspaper about a native who still lives in the eastern county, usually a frail but fierce old lady, clinging in spite of public outcry to her shabby house, raising a few chickens within yards of the pouring traffic.

In 1820 James Monroe was wearing knee breeches and buckled shoes in the White House and the Civil War was still forty years in the future, and the population of the county was 23,000. In 1960, when John F. Kennedy was elected president, it was still 23,000. In 1995 it topped 110,000 and double that expected within the next five years, with sixty thousand new houses scheduled.

The first new people came slowly, in the early '70s, and bought houses that were already here and moved in among the natives because they wanted to live in a place like this. They wanted to grow organic vegetables. They fixed the porch steps on the old house and rototilled the garden; their children joined 4-H and fit neatly into schools that were already here. The core population was dense enough to exert a gravitational pull and the first new people were easily attached to it.

The natives have always been pragmatic, but these former new people were romantics. They liked the old things and the old ways. They researched the original builders of the blacksnake-infested stone houses they'd bought. Some of the women took up spinning and weaving the wool from their own sheep. Now they're the preservationists among us, quick to take action when development threatens a historic bridge or a Civil War battlefield. They're the ones the developers call "elitist." We trust them to fight our fights.

Then the new international airport bloomed on the eastern edge of the county and brought with it our first public sewage system. As everywhere, public sewage was followed by housing developments, as if the developers had crawled in through

. . . . . .

the pipes. Land values jumped and taxes followed them. Farmers struggled and then gave in. Farms yielded to what were called "planned communities," an oxymoron.

These new new people in the developments don't want to live like the old ones. They're here to escape from the burglars back where they came from, but they want here to look and feel as much like there as possible, tidy, regulated, predictable. Convenient to shopping. They apparently considered secondhand houses as shameful as secondhand clothes, and knew without looking that a house that was already here wouldn't have half enough bathrooms.

Out here in the west, though, natives are still the dominant species and the pickup trucks outnumber the Volvos. For a long time, except when we noticed new houses crusting over the hill where the peach orchard used to be, we lived as if the commuters didn't exist.

We only noticed them when they voted to spend money. They did vote, invisibly, very early on their way east or very late on their way back, and the next day indignation rocked the tavern: Who *are* these people? How can there be so many of them? How did they get here, who invited them? Why do they need all those new schools; what happened to the schools we built them last year and why does a high school need tennis courts? Why do they have such expensive taste in toys?

The new people don't go hunting, fishing, or camping; they never sling a canoe on the car and head for the river; they don't want their children playing unsupervised in the woods or ice-skating on the ponds. They need scheduled recreational programs for all their children, all the time. They need swimming pools, gyms, weight-training rooms, bike

. . . . . .

trails, lighted soccer fields, and indoor sports arenas where grown-up commuters can play by night.

The new people are desperate for exercise. The natives feel that anyone who needs further exercise after the workday must be goofing off on the job. In fact, they find the whole concept of exercise absurd, even when they aren't being taxed for its facilities.

And so the tavern would grumble and the rift deepen, at least among the natives — the new people, passing through in the dark, probably didn't notice.

Except at elections, we tried to forget them. How can you keep on thinking about people you never see? Perhaps they didn't really exist. Or, if they did, perhaps they'd just slip away, back where they came from, as silently as they arrived. It was easy to ignore invisible people, and easy to forget what happened to the east, since we never went there anymore.

Most of the time it was easy to believe that we'd never wake up some morning surrounded, outnumbered, and supplanted by people in suits. Never find ourselves as invisible tomorrow as the commuters are today, or the Indians were yesterday.

Two years ago we held the racetrack referendum. An entrepreneur wanted to build a racetrack in the east. Here in the west there was great rejoicing over a market for our hay. We have a lot of hay. After the farmers' sons have given up serious farming and no longer keep grazing beasts or feed them over the winter, the fields still have to be cut or they'd grow up, not into hardwood forests, but into brambles and cedar scrub, plainly visible to the neighbors and a burning shame to the idle, feckless owner. So every June the hay is

. . . . . .

cut and rolled up into giant Shredded-Wheat rolls and stacked at the side of the highway with a black-and-red tin For Sale sign on it.

Nobody buys it. In a rainy season all that sweet, nourishing hay slowly turns black and begins to sprout green fuzz, no good for anything but mulch, and nobody buys it for mulch either. Presently it has to be hauled away somewhere, to make room for the late-summer cutting. It's sad to watch it thrown away, and sadder still for the owner. A racetrack would buy it.

Everyone in the west wanted a racetrack; nobody in the east did. In the east they saw it as flagrant corruption for their teenagers, who would certainly drop out of school to hang around the track and gamble away their lunch money.

The voter turnout for the referendum, a single-item ballot, was close to 100 percent. The whole west voted yes; the whole east voted no. The east won. I'm sorry to say some easterners, who don't seem to have been raised right, wrote gloating letters to the paper telling us we might as well not bother to vote anymore, not on local issues, because they had the numbers to cancel anything we wanted.

Probably by now they've forgotten it, over in the victorious east, but, as with the Civil War, the vanquished remember.

Jokes in the west about secession turned into serious consideration. The rift, fairly amiable before, became a chasm, and the county, which was always simply "the county" when I came five years before, is now always specified as the "eastern" or "western" county by the newspaper and the politicians. We don't consider the east properly *county* at all anymore; statistically it's become part of what's called the "metropolitan area," a concept hard to love. The two sections

· · · · · ·

no longer have anything in common, not even weather; schools in the western half keep having to close for snow.

The telephone company has confirmed the rift by changing our area code. The new people have bought so many car phones and beepers and computer modems that our old area code bulged at the seams, so we in the west have been cut off at the county seat and lumped together with the still-rural land of mid-Virginia. Muttering, we crossed out the phone numbers on our business cards and repainted the doors of our trucks, but secretly most of us here were pleased that Bell Atlantic joined us to the rotary-dial rubes where we belong.

This year the question on the table is a shopping mall. Not an ordinary mall, but what they're calling a "regional" mall, enormous, sprawling over many hundreds of acres. The east is surprised that we, who won't be affected by the traffic, are against it; they, who will have to live with the traffic, consider it a highly acceptable trade-off. Right in their own backyards, instead of useless fields and the threat of wildlife, they can have tanning salons, nail clinics, Weight Watchers, herbal body lotions, New Age crystals, computer enhancements, discount fashions, karate classes, Spandex biking shorts, and designer sunglasses.

They'll get them, of course. We are the past, as in "pastoral," and will never win another zoning battle. They are the now. Already invisibility is creeping over us. One of these days we'll be indistinguishable from the ghosts of Mosby's Rangers, or the nomadic Manahoac who disappeared when the buffalo left.

prior tenants

. . . .

They slewed the pickup into the drive, slithering ruts of mud, and tramped up the lawn in mud and snow — I was watching from the window — and banged on the back door. Both were handsome square-set men with wavy black hair and rotten teeth. Both wore dirty sweatshirts under red-and-black wool shirts. The leader said, "You're Missus Kelly? Or maybe Sprigg? Or Spragg?"

"No," I said.

He stepped back on my snowy steps a pace or two and faced me with wide-set eyes. "Harrison fixed it," he said. "You know Harrison? Right here, over next to where he hunts over that way. Kelly, he said."

"Nobody named Kelly on land anywhere around here."

"Harrison sent us on up. Said it was okay we could hunt."

They're plainly from west of here, in the hardscrabble hills where nobody could ever raise a decent crop. It's a Celtic look — mountainy — a look that spawned racist superstitions on the English edge of Wales. Not malevolent, but by no means tame. Maybe they have wives and children, but it's hard to imagine.

Politely, they've left their guns in the truck. It's basic manners not to come to the door with a gun on your shoulder.

"Hey," I protest. "Over that way and on down the mountain, that's Truesdell land. Harrison hunts there. Up there's Arndt, he's got a friend hunts it. Over that way is Elrod, nobody hunts his land. Maybe you mean the other side of the road." I am obscurely uncomfortable. These men are from an alien culture and I would like them off my land.

"Harrison said it was here."

"You want to call him?"

"Yes, ma'am." He sends his friend back to wait in the truck and smacks the push-button phone manfully.

"Tell him you're at Holland's place."

He does. Harrison sets him straight. "Missed it by three lanes," he says. "It's back down that way. Spragg was the name, if I'm saying it right. Sorry for your trouble, ma'am."

"No problem. Good hunting."

"Yes, ma'am, it is." And he goes away.

Populations here grind together like tectonic plates. Just to my east and creeping closer, men who carry umbrellas, women with law degrees. In the valley, the sons of farmers, keeping busy with various jobs. Behind my shoulder blades, across this mountain and into the next range, and on from there, the men who came to the door; secret people who never get counted in magazine articles about the way America lives; people who might appear at the edges of a regional novel but would never be taken seriously, or seriously believed to exist at all in the modern world. And just south of the next gap in the Blue Ridge, rich people who breed Thoroughbreds

. . . . . .

and give charity balls. All of us living in the same time and almost the same space. Things are more complicated than they look.

And underneath and around us all and sometimes visible, the original inhabitants, the creatures.

Only Bruce hunts my land, and he hunts with a bow like a gentleman. I trust him with my deer. Bruce is head photographer at the newspaper and very good; he might get rich and famous somewhere else, but he'd rather stay here and go hunting. Besides, his wife trains horses. He's from the far east, from Tidewater country, a Scot and a Saxon, not a Celt. (How far back in time do prejudices run, and how many people of British descent would rather buy a used car from a blue-eyed blond?)

Bruce wants to shoot my turkeys in the spring, but I like having them here. Sometimes when I round the bend in the lane, the whole flock is standing there blocking my way, conferring in shocked undertones for all the world like a DAR meeting rejecting an applicant.

Besides, as far as I know, they don't eat tomatoes.

IT WAS PIGHEADED of me to want to grow tomatoes outdoors, and I don't know why I kept trying. I coddled their seedlings on windowsills; I set them outside and tended them obsessively; every year others ate them first. I have never bitten into a tomato grown in my own soil.

Now, on the deck, ten feet above deer and rabbit level, I grow tomatoes, peppers, basil, lettuce, and parsley. They live in tubs and pots and window boxes, in expensive potting soil bought from the hardware store and hauled home, watered by hand, and fertilized artificially. I resent this. I might as

· · · · · ·

well live in the city and garden on a balcony. All those acres of perfectly good dirt out there, and I pay taxes on this dirt, and I'm not allowed a single salad from it.

In my first, most optimistic year, I planted two apple trees, expensive little sprouts of an ancient lineage. As soon as they leafed out the following spring, deer ate them down to nubbins. Deer eat the plants from the top down. Raccoons dig them up, curious about what's under their roots, and leave them to wilt. Possums and groundhogs pull each tomato off as it ripens and maul it, before they climb the peach tree to take a single bite out of each ripening peach. This year, before the raccoons, before the peaches were ripe, my merry trio of squirrels, who work and play and chatter together like an early Disney cartoon, stripped the entire peach tree between night and morning, leaving not a single peach as a memorial to what would have been a bumper crop. Since peaches can't be stored like acorns, I can only suppose the squirrels are making peach brandy. Maybe they'll sell me some.

I think about putting up an eight-foot chain-link fence with a latched gate. Then I think about a groundhog burrowing briskly under the fence and a raccoon fiddling intelligently with the latch. I also remember a neighbor, back in Pennsylvania, who built such a fence and woke one morning to find that a doe and her two youngsters had jumped in and, without room for a take-off run, found themselves trapped and panicked, trampling what they hadn't eaten into a wallow of greenish mud.

Mostly I try to consider my acreage purely aesthetic and myself a squatter on land that rightfully belongs to the permanent occupants, the creatures that lived here first.

There are creatures aplenty. Whitetail deer, first and

· · · · · ·

foremost, their numbers swelling annually, crowding them from the country into towns and suburbs where they crash through glass doors and wander bemused on highways and airport runways. However many move to town, though, I still have plenty on the mountain.

Four years ago I planted a row of azaleas across the back of the house. They were knee-high when I planted them. They still are, though the mountain laurel at the end of the row is noticeably smaller than it was. Occasionally a single flower appears, low down against the wall, the more convenient buds having been bitten off just as they swelled toward blooming. Sometimes, brushing my teeth at the bathroom window, I find myself eyeball to eyeball with the culprits and run out yelling.

I don't make a very frightening figure, I'm afraid. My deer actually seem quite fond of me and ignore my shouts and police whistle and flung sticks as if I were a child in a tantrum. I flail at them, cursing like a fishwife, and they come toward me, cheerful and friendly, looking aristocratic as a herd of countesses, their slim faces delicately modeled, their dark eyes calm, until I can almost touch them.

Once you're that close to a deer it's hard to stay angry. This is why deer have overrun the mid-Atlantic; we'd never allow warthogs to multiply so freely. I find myself smiling, and the broom I was brandishing drops feebly: "Aw, well. Good morning to you, too, then."

In winter, in fresh snow, deer tracks are crisscrossed with other, larger tracks. Bobcat? And whose footprints are those, that look like a giant's zipper across the yard? I must get a book on tracks. Last winter, unmistakable bear prints circled the house, passing so close to the back door that their maker must have considered knocking on it for a handout. I was pleased and excited to have a bear, until I followed the tracks to the lower porch and considered the remains of the trash bags. Among the strewn litter of crushed cans and coffee grounds the bear, like a psychotic burglar, had defecated copiously. Too late I realized he had also urinated on the woodpile; when I tossed a log onto a roaring fire the smell sent the cats howling out of the room.

One night I opened the door to let a cat out, and up on the snow-covered slope twenty yards away, the cat and I saw two bright yellow lights, like the headlights of a low-slung sports car. They blinked out, leaving darkness, then on again; moved a few feet away and turned themselves to focus unwinking on us in the doorway.

I snatched up the cat and went back inside.

This year, maybe I'll give up on tomatoes. Resign myself, not from ecological sentiment but from common sense. I am outnumbered here, a trespasser with no natural rights to this land.

Just the same, if they won't let me grow tomatoes, I wish they'd chip in on the taxes.

AT LEAST the mice moved out.

The mice lived in the crawl space between ceiling and roof, and they'd lived there for countless mouse generations while the house stood empty except in summer. When I moved in full-time and turned on the heat, there must have been general rejoicing. True, I'd brought a cat, but Morgan was a poor excuse for a predator. Once in a while she'd carry

. . . . . .

a mouse around, looking proud and motherly, and put it down to pat and play with for a few minutes, but then she'd lose interest and the mouse would go on home. Twice, in the middle of the night, she brought one to bed, slipping it in all warm and wriggly under my bare foot.

Any temporary inconvenience she offered the mice was amply repaid by the miraculous new supply of dry cat food or, from their point of view, mouse food, conveniently set out in a bowl. Prudently, in case the gods changed their minds, the mice set up emergency caches of cat food all over the house. Dry, crunchy cat food in my boots, cat food in the cups in the china cupboard, cat food in the linen closet and the silverware drawer. I opened the folding bed for guests and a rattling shower of cat chow poured out.

The mice came and went by way of a narrow crack where the stone chimney meets the ceiling, squeezing their fat compressible bodies in and out, like pushing a marsh-mallow through a wedding ring. One that I thought of as Hickory-Dickory ran the length of the living room every night at eleven o'clock, scampered up the stones, and squeezed through the crack. Once, with every sign of har-ried impatience, he ran over a guest's foot rather than de-tour around it.

The cat sat on the mantelpiece and watched the crack. One evening a mouse slid down onto her face, astonishing both. Vindicated, she went on watching, and ten minutes later a second mouse fell on her face. A good time was had by all. Then Pickett moved in, a mountain cat with a firmer grasp of his mission in life. All cats are not equal, mousewise. The first evening he caught and ate a mouse in the bedroom, washed up, and went out to the kitchen and caught and ate another mouse. In the morning he corraled a mouse in the bathtub and ate it.

The survivors moved out. Overnight they abandoned their ancestral home. Fancifully I thought of tiny suitcases being dragged across the attic floor, tiny taxis pulling up at the door. One day there had been a mouse in every kitchen drawer; the next day they'd left nothing behind but their stashes of cat chow and a litter of droppings in the oven.

I was pleased in a way — they'd seemed impossible to toilet train — but it was verging on winter, and these mice had led a sheltered life. Would they manage on their own in the woods? After all, they were here before I was, and I felt a certain dim responsibility to the local wildlife, the prior tenants.

Then I forgot them as the various problems of the mountain winter took over. For one thing, my car heater stopped working. For a while it made a rustling sound, like a snake on dry leaves, and then it quit altogether. My feet got colder and colder and finally, exasperated, I popped the hood and looked in. I rarely do this because, except for the windshield-washer jug, I don't know what those things are in there and they make me feel ignorant and foolish. This time, though, I knew just what I was looking at. Acorns. Hundreds and hundreds of acorns, heaped and piled and tucked into every cranny. I gathered up as many as I could reach, filling a standard grocery bag, and dumped them under the oak tree where they belonged. However, this had nothing to do with the heater, which still didn't work, so I took the car to the dealer.

Waiting, I settled down in the lounge area to read dog-eared copies of *Road and Track*. Presently the service manager opened the door and stared compellingly in at me. "Would you come with me, please?" he said. "I want to show you something."

Nervous, I jumped up. "It wouldn't be something about — uh, about *acorns* — would it?" He didn't answer. He led me to my car.

The mechanic was crouched on the floor with his head under the dashboard, cursing softly but sincerely to himself. He'd pulled the heater's hose connection apart, and a firmly packed fibrous lump bulged out through the gap. He was picking at it with his fingers, pulling out bits of fuzz. Not acorns, but the stringy lining or trashy bits left over when you've finished eating the best part of the acorn. My tidy guests kept their groceries piled up all over, but they stashed their garbage neatly in the heater hose. The mechanic, arduously trained in the most sophisticated, computerized mysteries of the modern car, spent forty minutes teasing it out, and the expression on his face was dark and complicated.

The bill was discreetly worded. "Repair heater" was all it said. Here, even my car is habitat.

LAST FALL the house inexplicably, in a matter of minutes, filled up with a swarm of ladybugs. I scooped them from the windows and the sink and the bathtub and tried to throw them out the door but more flew in. I couldn't help stepping on them, leaving mournful red stains on the floor. Days later I was still plucking them from the curtains and off the leftovers in the refrigerator.

The county is full of creatures, great and small. As the

· · · · · ·

valley fills up with inhospitable houses and lawns, I suppose my mountain will be their last home.

INEXPLICABLY, though, as civilization moves in from the east, more unsuitable wildlife moves in, presumably from the western wilderness, and the two converge. Black bears appear in the streets of the county seat and on the runways of the airport.

In July, I was lounging on the deck on a bright Saturday afternoon, soaking in the scarce sunshine of a foggy summer, my cats sprawled around me. I was vaguely aware of coughing, chuffing noises in the woods, but many things chuff in my woods. Then the cats sprang to the alert. Pickett slunk to the edge of the deck and peered around toward the back of the house, every muscle rigid with outrage. "What's up, Pick?" I asked. "Who's out there?" He mumbled something hostile deep in his throat.

I went in through the house and out the kitchen door, onto the back steps, and there she was. On the lawn, by the clothesline. My first thought was, "Oh, it's Elsa!"

A mountain lion doesn't look like anything except a lion, though smaller than the ones in the zoo. There's no missing the rounded ears, the broad flat nose, the powerful forelegs, the imperious tawny eye. "Well, hello there," I said.

We considered each other levelly. Then slowly, almost reluctantly, she turned and started up the grass path, pausing from time to time to look over her shoulder at me. She sprang up onto the stone row, right where the red fox sat last winter, and turned to stare down at the house. I had the uneasy feeling that she'd bought the place and was waiting for me to pack and leave.

· · · · · ·

Prior Tenants 185

I went back to the deck to soothe my cats, but they were unsoothed. The coughing sounds resumed, this time with a touch of a snarl, and kept circling the house possessively.

Several nights later, I had just settled into bed with a book when she screamed in through the bedroom window. I suppose the correct word would be "bloodcurdling." I had read, in Westerns, that a mountain lion screams like a woman, but it's been years since I heard a woman scream and this sounded more like a five-hundred-pound peacock in a rage.

Not to be bullied in my own bed, I pressed my forehead to the screen and screamed back until my throat burned. Silence. Then, just as I reopened my book, she screamed in through the kitchen window. She must have been close. She must have been standing in the azaleas, possibly with her front paws on the windowsill.

It was a long time before I could concentrate on reading.

For a week my own cats refused to leave the house without me.

I wanted to tell someone, but I was cautious. After all, she was my guest, and I didn't want her hassled. Besides, officially there are no mountain lions here, and haven't been for generations, and reporting one is like reporting your abduction by space aliens. Finally I settled on a local wildlife expert.

She was pleased, of course, but baffled by its odd behavior. "You don't *see* mountain lions," she said, "until they're on top of you. They're wary. This one might have been somebody's pet, there's quite a black market in big cats. Then it got too big and they ditched it. In that case, it wouldn't have any fear of humans..."

We both knew what this meant. When I left, in the dark, she said, "If the lion's there, just stay in your car till it goes away." Oh. Well, yes. Somehow a lion by night is different from a lion in the sunlight. When I got home, instead of leaving the car in the driveway I drove clear across the lawn and parked at the kitchen door.

A few weeks later I went out to gather catnip. Catnip grows freely all across the sweep of woods and wildflowers behind the house, and it has been my custom to gather it and dry it and make it into cat toys. At least, I made toys for a while, whimsical felt mice with painted faces and yarn tails, but then I decided I wasn't the crafts type and just stuffed it into red socks and knotted them. At Christmas I passed these out among cat-owning friends.

Not this year, though. It was gone. All of it. The patch by the walnut tree, the patch by the stone row, the patch by the raspberries . . . Not a leaf. Not a twig.

I remembered once hearing that when the federal government was trying to wipe out big cats in the West, they baited their traps with catnip, which seems unsporting. I had neglected the trap, but I'd certainly spread out the bait.

Not necessarily fearless because of being somebody's pet, then. Fearless because stoned out of her mind. Drugged to the whiskers.

I can't decide whether to plant more. Who will come? The last tigers, flying in from Bengal?

A SMALL BAND OF good-hearted local people have formed a wildlife-habitat conservancy. I sit on their board and write their press releases and their newsletter, happy to feel busy and useful though secretly I know the cause is as lost as that other mourned Cause. Our object is to persuade the new people in the housing developments to make some space for

• • • • • •

creatures; not to mow their lawns so tidily; to leave a corner of their land in wildflowers for the birds and butterflies. To persuade developers to leave strips of tall grass and bushes around the ponds and creeks.

Every third Tuesday we arrange lectures and slide shows at the main library, attended by ourselves and a handful of those who already believe, already plant coneflowers. Experts come to explain stream-ecology management to us, and how to tell a red-tailed from a sharp-shinned hawk. We in the audience make sketches and take notes and then serve punch and homemade cookies.

The natives don't come. They already know all there is to know about their wildlife, though they're apt to think of it as either food or varmints, and a butterfly garden would embarrass them horribly.

The developers don't come. Aside from living prudently far away, they have a vendetta against the deer that eat their rows of store-bought evergreens decorating the developments' gateways.

The new people don't come. I expect the thought of attracting instead of repelling wildlife would sound like madness to them.

They see nature in general as a threat, as somehow unnatural. They pass laws about keeping the lawns shaved short in case nature should creep in under cover. They write angry letters to the paper about mice and ants in the kitchen; they feel someone should do something.

Last summer a skunk wandered into one of the new developments. Several people looked out their windows and saw it meandering across the back lawns. They called Animal Control, but Animal Control said it was responsible for stray

dogs, not wild animals. Furious, they called the sheriff's office. The sheriff's office said it didn't have the staff to go
chasing skunks, and to leave it alone and it would go away.

Phone calls flew back and forth, and finally a man in the
neighborhood was persuaded to bring over his bedside re-
volver. Intrepid homeowners managed to coax the skunk into
an overturned garbage can, wherein the man shot him half a
dozen times. The next issue of the paper was scorched at its
edges from the letters: it was the basic duty of the county
government to protect its citizens, and if the current sheriff
was too lazy to do so, just wait till he saw what happened
come election time.

Almost immediately an enterprising fellow started a private
wildlife control business. Call him, and for a price he will
come and cope. He will have plenty to cope with. Our many-
toothed but inoffensive possum with its long bare tail causes
the most panic and is usually described, hysterically, as a
monstrous great rat with fangs.

One woman recently come from away wrote to the paper
to say that her former neighbors had warned her about the
intrusive creatures in this outlying county, but she hadn't realized just how bad it was going to be. She has had flies in
her guest room, wasps in her attic, and a stray cat in her
basement. Most alarming of all, in her three years here, five
birds have flown down her chimney to "terrorize not only our
infant son but also various Easter dinner guests."

She may have meant "terrify" rather than "terrorize," but
even so she seems to have fainthearted guests; most birds
small enough to fly down chimneys are easily overpowered
by adult humans.

She isn't giving up, though. She and thousands like her

. . . . . .

Prior Tenants 189

plan to stay and fight. I suppose the refugees will be starting up the mountain soon, possum and raccoon and groundhog, snake and butterfly, skunk and chickadee, doe and fawn and chipmunk, until my woods will look like the only hummock in a flooded lowland, where everything that walks or flies or creeps gathers to press together in the safety zone and wait for their homes to reappear behind them.

IT MAY BE RIGHT HERE, in my backyard, that everything will converge and the final battle will be fought. They'll all collide in a massive showdown, untamable mountain men with shotguns, rich folk on Thoroughbreds, farmers' sons on hay balers, suburbanites with cell phones, black bear, and mountain lion, all duking it out among my azaleas to settle the question of who shall inherit the Manahoac's hunting grounds.

coming soon

· · · · · · · · · · · · · · · · ·

Down in the valley the Christmas decorations go up early, to enjoy the longest possible run. They reflect a church-going population, with more lighted crèches out front than Santas. One family has a raft anchored in the middle of their farm pond, and early in December they row their crèche out to it, so that we who pass can admire it from the road. Surrounded by cold dark waters, the holy family looks precarious and brave.

Picket fences are entwined with holly branches. Lights are wound into the trees and across the front porches. Railings and pillars are wrapped in red ribbon. At great risk to life and limb, whole houses are outlined in lights — doors, windows, eaves, chimney, and roofline — so that by night they're a fragile picture of a house, drawn by a light pen. Even on the loneliest gravel road, houses wear their lighted Christmas trees in windows with the curtains open to cheer any possible wayfarer. On the road north to the Potomac a farmer pulls his hay cart out to the roadside and fills it with life-size wise men and shepherds.

Pickup trucks, being an extension of the home, almost an extension of the self, wear wreaths on their radiator grills, ribbons fluttering. The wreaths appear at the same time as the plow blades and the effect is both merry and self-sufficient, saying that here is a truck of goodwill and capability, offering travelers both season's greetings and emergency help. (In all seasons, many letters to the editor begin, "My family and I would like to thank the two men in the blue pickup who..." In blizzard and flood seasons, the feats are downright heroic.)

In December, all across the valley, a single candlelight burns in every window, so that the passerby feels welcomed, even expected. It's the same impulse that leads our citizens to plant their flower beds out beside road or sidewalk instead of along their own walls. A house, we feel, should say hello, assuming that even strangers are its friends. To the sophisticated, this seems a peculiarly public way to live, as if one's home weren't strictly private property at all but belonged to its world; as if the family weren't sealed inside it but promiscuously reaching out in all directions.

For Easter the raft people set up their giant rabbit, and thousands of colored eggs are painstakingly wired to the leafless trees in the front yards.

On Memorial Day, flags appear on front lawns and draped across the width of the barns, but the family has gone to the cemetery with trowel and clippers and potted plants to tend and decorate their graves, a ritual that must be growing rarer in a country where most of us live so far from the family

. . . . . .

bones. Here, though, graves are still part of the home — out-buildings, so to speak — and as such they should be decorated for all the living to enjoy.

The Fourth of July calls for patriotic bunting draped over the porch before everyone heads for the party, carrying folding chairs. The Fourth is as communal as Thanksgiving is famil-ial, with parade and picnic and softball game and the vol-unteer fire company in charge of fireworks. All are welcome.

Halloween is our most decorated season. Porches are piled with pumpkins and tall sheaves of cornstalks. Walks are lined with lighted jack-o'-lanterns and pots of yellow chrysanthe-mums; more chrysanthemums circle the mailbox posts. Sheet ghosts dangle from front-yard trees in a flutter of orange paper streamers, and life-size, homemade witches with real brooms loll drunkenly by the doorways. Fields are dedicated to pump-kin festivals, with pony rides, trestle tables of jack-o'-lanterns, homemade jellies and cookies for sale, and a mountain of newly harvested pumpkins sprawling over a corner of their field. Families pick through them. Each child chooses one to take home and carve and add to the row already on the porch. The jack-o'-lanterns face out toward the world, the way a snowman must always look at the street and not into the win-dows of its house.

At the fire company, the ladies' auxiliary takes charge of Halloween. Sometimes there's a small parade to show off the costumes before the auxiliary and firemen, dressed as ghosts or pirates, shepherd the young from decorated house to house and drive them to outlying homesteads, where front walks are outlined in jack-o'-lantern light. Householders who won't be available may drop off candy at the firehouse and the auxiliary

· · · · · ·

will pass it around. Nobody will check it for razor blades.

And so this antique way of life rolls through its ceremonious year, apparently never noticing how fragile it is or how soon it will grind to a stop and the decorations dwindle and move indoors, leaving only a wreath nailed to the door. Probably the porch chairs will go too.

Faith in the kindness of strangers collapses when strangers outnumber the neighbors ten to one, as they will in North Hill, pouring in like armies as the new development springs up overnight, the way developments do.

Writing in one of our free local tabloids, citizen Wayne Allensworth says anthropologists and sociologists agree that "altruistic behavior in human beings is encouraged by circumstances in which mutual recognition is possible. In other words, altruism is encouraged in face-to-face situations where people know one another and reciprocity is a real possibility. Recognition and mutual aid are the hallmarks of community." Human nature was designed to live in small groups. How big is too big? he asks, and answers that if you can visit the grocery store, the barbershop, or the pharmacy and not know anyone there, it's too big. Community fades and each man is an island.

Over the past seventy-five years, North Hill grew from 359 inhabitants to 530, including outlying farmers. The eleven hundred new houses to cover the land on the north and south will contain maybe five thousand strangers.

The project was inflaming citizens' meetings when I first came, six years ago now, and residents filed lawsuits claiming their wells would run dry, as indeed they may. The suits failed, of course, but an economic recession ran the project

· · · · · ·

into a bog of bankruptcies. The villagers and I forgot about it. Behind our backs it rose up again.

One of the developers told a reporter that there was nothing we could do but "relax and get used to it." I suppose it would be wicked to pray for another recession, another six years respite.

Gamely the villagers and the mayor have proclaimed their intention of making the newcomers welcome. The mayor has suggested laying sidewalks at the town's expense from the developments into the heart of North Hill, the diner, the firehouse, the post office. It's hard to imagine people using them, though. They'll need their own things, a new school of their own and a post office branch, since the North Hill post office has only three parking spaces, one of them for wheelchairs.

Nobody knows what will become of the volunteer fire and rescue. Everything will be different.

For the moment, however, we still live with the blind goodwill of very young children who have never been slapped or scolded, and offer a lick of our lollipop to everyone we see. We still deck our halls on the outside, with ribbons and boughs of holly for our friend the world to enjoy.

MY SISTER comes to visit, having business in the area, and we spend a happy, idle week driving around attending to matters beyond the mountains and south as far as Page Valley. I feel slightly feckless having a sister come from as far away as California, and explain to everyone that she and her husband are not really Californians but assigned there by the Park Service. This meets with approval: honest outdoor work.

Then she needs to be returned to the airport, forty-some

miles to the dangerous east. For the first time in months, I have ferreted out the alarm clock, plugged it in, and set it, musing on the word "alarm" and why the world must be wakened daily to cries of panic and danger.

It shrieks hideously in the dark. I drag myself out of bed and grope for light switches, bumping into Becky. "This is uncivilized," I mutter into my coffee. "Aren't there any planes at lunchtime?"

"Don't be a sissy. *Lots* of people get up this early. My friend Sue has to get up at four-fifteen. She commutes."

My cats are still in bed, entwined in blankets. The squadrons of birds who sponge off my feeder won't get up until eight; nine if it's cloudy.

The dark before dawn seems colder, more hostile, than darkness at midnight. "Black as the inside of a cow," my sister complains. I turn on the floodlight and we load the car with luggage and set forth, crunching frozen snow. The highway that crosses the Gap is usually so empty that I barely slow for the Stop sign, but this morning — if this is indeed morning — it's a pouring stream of headlights. "What's happening?" I ask, thinking sleepily of disasters to the west. Warfare, floods, pestilence, the population fleeing.

"Commuters."

I press down the gas pedal and merge among them, joining what must be half the population west of the mountain, all of us aimed southeasterly toward the city. As we pass the on-ramps to each town, more cars squeeze in; nobody gets off. Claustrophobia paralyzes me. By the time we pass the county seat, the highway is solid with what I take on faith, in the dark, to be cars; red lights rush away to the horizon. Between the lights rocket invisible tons of metal urged forward by angry, sleepy people in a desperate hurry. They have a long way to go, much farther than I do.

For the first time I turn off onto the new toll road, the state-of-the-art high-speed road that will carry commuters from the edge of Washington straight to our county seat, whence they can fan out to populate the countryside beyond.

A thin fog starts to freeze on the back window, and I punch the defroster. No sign of day lights the east.

When I lived in the city I walked to work. By daylight. In deepest winter I walked home in what passes for darkness in the city, under streetlights, past lighted shops and restaurants. When I was married, my husband kept a car in a garage; we took it out on weekends to visit friends. And back in my suburban childhood, back when suburbs meant rosebushes and boredom and a place where the children could play outdoors, my father walked to the avenue to catch a bus to work and walked home in the evening from the bus stop bearing a well-chilled evening paper. My mother used the car for grocery shopping.

"These people go through this *every day?* A job would have to be terribly exciting and *terribly* well-paid..."

"They hardly notice," says Becky callously. "They used to live closer in, and just kept gradually moving farther and farther out so they had time to adjust."

Surely this is madness? Surely, once upon a time, office and factory workers lived in the city and farmers lived in the country, trains and trolley cars stitched the world together, and a car was a kind of toy, to take out for a drive on Sunday?

And what of that train we used to have? The Washington and Old Dominion line pushed all the way to the Blue Ridge in 1898. It ran passenger service and local and through freight

· · · · · ·

Coming Soon 197

trains and a special milk train known as the Virginia Creeper. It brought the mail and the sweaty city folk, come for fresh air, and going back it carried our excellent milk, live calves, and wheat from the fields; in little Pikesville the stone grain elevator still stands below the highway, a mystery to commuters. The train made twenty-one stops in our county alone, but service began to limp in the 1940s, and by 1951 even the mail contract was canceled.

Just recently a lot of its old roadbed has been converted to a bicycle and jogging trail. Everyone is pleased and proud, and there's been much self-congratulation over this triumph of health and ecology. A preservation society has converted our former train station into a tiny museum to lure tourists, with available toilets for bicycle riders.

Under my tires, fourteen miles of good dirt six lanes wide will never see sunlight again, and all around me stream the countless thousands of unfortunates who live this nightmare twice a day. With so many of them, surely if they joined forces they could move back to the withering cities and forge them into safe and vigorous places to live? Places where they could rise up by daylight and take the subway, sit down at their desks twenty minutes later, smiling and sane? In other countries the cities grow and grow. In Paris and London, Venice and Rome, the richer and more important you are, the closer you live to the pulsing heart of town, and the suburbs are scorned as a banishment for the unworthy.

Rearranging the world in my mind, I almost miss the airport exit. To judge from the crush at the terminal, many people nowadays *fly* to work every morning. Leaving, I can't shoehorn myself into the far left lane to the new on-ramp and have to take the long way around.

· · · · · ·

Slowly, as I head back west, the black morning begins to turn gray. My side of the road is almost empty; the other side still pours headlights. In front of me the Blue Ridge takes shape against the sky. By the time full daylight comes, my gentle valley will have drained off all its important people. At the diner, the long table will be occupied by men in jeans and down vests; the waitress will move around them refilling their coffee mugs. Scattered pickup trucks will travel the highway with dogs in their passenger seats.

When I get home, disoriented by my trip through the future, the first birds have gathered at the feeder. The cats are still asleep. I wind the cord around the alarm clock and put it away, make more coffee and, before I start work, pause to feel amazingly, dazzlingly, almost uniquely blessed by the life I'm managing to live.

the end of the world
··················

Summer before last I wasted a lot of time standing on the deck looking out over the valley. I wanted to remember it carefully.

It looked much like this in the early 1700s. The dairy cows were gone but their pastures were still there, cut for hay now, and the woodlots and the smooth sweet hills rolling away toward the sunrise and a silo here and there.

Last spring the road people finished the final stretch of four-lane, and before the asphalt was dry the signs had sprung up in the fields on either side. "Future Site of Hunt Country Homes," they said, and "Coming: Heritage Farms," and "Mountainvue Estates — Affordably Priced Executive Living."

In the summer I could see five big fields and in the winter, with the leaves off the trees, seven. Every year they turned from green to tawny to white to green. By this time next year, each field will be covered with homes. I can no longer refer to the new people in the east; they'll be here in the west, clear up against the Blue Ridge itself. "The bulldozers are coming," as one county official put it, "and all you can do is get out of their way."

Samples have already been built. I can see them. For the first time I can see new houses without binoculars. Well, of course I can see them; they're enormous. I tend to think of the new people as being several times as big as the rest of us, needing houses for giants. My whole house — not even a developer would call it a "home" — could hide in one of their master bathrooms, and their assertive bulk and sprawling garages bury the pasture grass. The garages alone are enough to confuse the eye; much as we love our cars here, it hadn't occurred to us to build them special housing, attached to our rooms and opened electronically so that no one need ever go outdoors at all.

Sometimes, driving absentmindedly, I round a bend and see a hillside of new houses and for a minute can't understand what these objects are, what they're *for.* My eyes have been full of our local houses for so long, houses no bigger than necessary and, on farms, dwarfed by barns and silos. Plain houses.

Some of the new houses try to look like farmhouses, only they're blown up to several times their normal size and look bloated. In more ambitious developments, each new house is an architectural encyclopedia of Palladian windows, faux Tudor timbering, antebellum plantation pillars, Norman towers, New England widow's walks, and medieval doors through which four horsemen in full armor could ride abreast.

There's plenty of construction work available now, and everyone here seems to know how to hang Sheetrock and nail trim. The farmers' sons are building houses for the new people so the farmers' grandsons can mow their lawns and fry

. . . . . .

their hamburgers, like the bemused subjects of a colonial power come from away to take charge.

I read in the city paper of a peaceful tribe of Indians in Brazil, squeezed off their ancestral land, who are devastating their numbers in an epidemic of suicides. Anthropologist Alcida Ramos, in his book *Indigenous Societies*, writes, "Land is much more than simply a means of subsistence. It is the support for a social life that is directly linked to their system of belief and knowledge."

EARLY ON, it was felt that the aesthetically and ecologically correct way to sell off a farm was in ten-acre lots with a house in the middle of each and its own asphalt drive to the road. The results look peculiarly desolate and still refuse to blend in. They seem to have no reason to be where they are rather than elsewhere, or nowhere.

The newest concept to catch our fancy is what we're calling the "rural village." Instead of a moonscape of huge houses on huge lots, houses will be planted in clusters on small lots, since busy commuters have no use for land anyway, and the rest of the farm shall be left as open space. The phrase "open space" falls soothingly on the ear, as it was designed to do. The new people in the new houses can decide whether to picnic on it, or play baseball, or divide it into vegetable plots, or leave it alone. This cooperative property will draw the strangers together in merry fellowship until they bond and form a community, like the villagers of old, though it might seem to the curmudgeonly just as likely to tear them apart in dissension.

Who can quarrel with open space? No one wants to say that this is not prairie or desert but generously fertile and

. . . . . .

watered ground, and unless it's mowed or grazed or planted, in its first season what was pasture and cornfield will be an impenetrable jungle of brush and brambles. I know. It happens to me every spring. Blackberries will flourish where no one can reach to pick them, and poison ivy and the wickedly thorned multiflora rose, the dense, spiny Japanese privet, sumac, ailanthus, and our scrubby sassafras that lured early entrepreneurs to the county, back when its bark was considered a cure for syphilis. Neither woodland nor farmland but what the survey reports called "waste land," the open space will be useful only to the unwelcome. Raccoons, always presumed to be rabid, will come forth to rattle the garbage cans and frighten the children.

Big houses on big square lawns were a lousy idea. Open space is a lousy idea too. Cities were a good idea, and so were farms and farming towns, but their time seems to have passed. I can't think of any new good ideas.

By last summer's end there were eight or ten big new houses, still widely scattered across my slice of view, the forerunners.

HIDDEN FROM where I stand on the mountain, down in the folds of the valley, are four small towns not greatly changed since the Civil War, except for some shrinkage. Farming towns don't grow the way suburbs grow. Now they crouch there, frozen like rabbits in the headlights of executive homes.

If only the builders could build another town or two. Maybe with a white church steeple pointing up. But nobody's going to build a town. Nobody can, except perhaps on a studio back lot; a town has to grow organically out of things people need, and nobody needs a town anymore. All we need is a place to sleep and a place to work and a six-lane highway between them, with an off-ramp to the shopping mall.

River and harbor towns grew up because of rivers and harbors. Our towns grew up because of farms. Where the soil was rich and deep, the towns prospered along with the farmers, and our valley soil has been praised since the first white man stuck his fingers into it. Our farmers tended it respectfully, nourished it with cover crops, and raised plenty of livestock for manure. Where the bulldozers scrape off its skin, like peeling the frosting off a cake, its goodness cries out for seeds.

WHEN THE COUNTRY was young, the fertility of the land meant everything. It was the answer to whether you settled here or moved on and kept looking. The firstcomers picked the most generous soil; the latecomers pushed on, pausing to pick up a handful of dirt and smell it and crumble it between their fingers, considering, looking around for an all-weather spring, maybe a creek where the pasture would be. Now fertility means only that the farmers on good land are the last to sell to developers, holding out, scratching a living, while the hardscrabble people, however sadly, sold early. Now land is nothing but location, which means nothing but driving to an office: how far, how fast. Rich soil is nothing but a firm surface on which to set a house.

All over the country — all over the world, I suppose — you can tell by the towns and houses and faces what kind of dirt's under your feet. In farming country, even postfarming country, it shows in the faces. Drive west from here to the humped fields scabbed over with rocks too big to blast and thin gray

. . . . . .

grass that would hardly nourish a nanny goat, or out to the dry country where the topsoil blows away after it's plowed, or north to the short growing seasons where the dirt barely has a chance to warm up before frost, and you're in a land of narrow-hipped houses, because wood is scarce and heat rises, and suspicious faces. Thick rock and thin topsoil make harsh people. Where a person's parents and grandparents had to work too hard for too little, they worked the children hard too, and laid into them with a heavy hand when they shirked their chores. There was no time for games or flowers. Worry pinches the cheeks and sours the mind. The towns there look closed even when they're open. Nobody smiles.

Good dirt makes happy people. It grows farm towns with wide porches and flourishing gardens and cheerful children. Stunted towns from shallow soil; blossoming towns from deep dirt. Our dirt was good. It's still good, but it isn't useful anymore.

THE SEED OF a town was a farmer who needed a mill to grind his grain and a blacksmith to shoe his horses and mend his wagon wheels. The miller and the smith set up shop in the most convenient place and built their houses. The farmers' families needed salt and sugar, needles and thread and yard goods, hats and boots. The storekeeper and the shoemaker moved in next to the miller and the smith, because the roads didn't encourage driving hither and yon to shop. The post office moved in among the yard goods. The tavern opened.

With the necessities in place, everyone pitched in and built a schoolhouse and a church with a house for the preacher and space for a graveyard, and there it was: a town. An anchor.

. . . . . .

A place to collect your mail and lean against the shop fronts chatting with your far-flung neighbors, trading the gossip of crops and pigs, and feeling less alone in the world.

Each valley town developed a distinctive flavor, depending on its constituents. You can still feel the difference — a plain-spoken, no-nonsense town settled by German refugees from the Palatinate wars; a peaceable, sequestered town settled by Quakers from Pennsylvania; and the richest town, on the trading road to the west, with its big stone houses now taken over by outlanders with the money to restore them.

My own little Pikestown down at the foot of the Gap was a way station for travelers resting up before or after crossing the mountain. The young George Washington bedded there whenever he was in the neighborhood surveying. The wagon men needed food and drink and beds, hay for their horses. I understand it got pretty noisy on a Saturday night. During the Civil War its position as guardian of the Gap made it even noisier, and many a minor skirmish echoed on its two steep streets.

They aren't important, of course, these towns, and they've served their purpose. For human friendliness, I'm told over and over again that Americans have re-created the gossipy intimacy of small towns by using the Internet. For shopping, we can drive swiftly and easily to the big chain stores over to the east.

Through the efforts of our early, earnest newcomers, mills and churches, roads and whole villages get themselves onto various historic registers, to be preserved like fossil footprints in volcanic rock, and preserved is better than destroyed but not the same as useful.

The shopping streets in the county seat are quiet. The

. . . . . .

town's elders are struggling to fill them with tourists, because only tourists can save them now. The National Trust for Historic Preservation sponsors a Main Street program, under which towns are supposed to bloom again by enhancing their history, restoring their Victorian facades, and replacing their plain street signs with curly, old-fashioned ones. We try. Press releases are sent out calling the place historic and quaint. Craft fairs and history tours and Colonial Days are staged, with balloons and funnel cakes for sale on the sidewalks. New businesses are encouraged to open and sell basketry, gifts, T-shirts, and antiques to strangers in the same shops that once sold yard goods and nails to neighbors. The new shops are run by people from away, since the natives find it hard to adjust, and they don't last long. There aren't enough tourists.

Occasionally I see a pair of them, or a pair of pairs, on Market Street peering in the windows of the three little restaurants or prodding the earrings and dishware in the antique shop. They seem bewildered, as if wondering why they drove so far to such an unremarkable place. This is a good place to live but a bad place to visit. There's nothing to do. We have a county museum in a little log cabin, but it doesn't take long to look at the old farm tools and photographs and pick through the pamphlets on local history.

Word has just come in to the newspaper that the bank across from the courthouse is leaving its gabled Victorian building and moving out to the shopping mall on the highway. Nobody knows what's to become of the building. It's too big and dignified to sell T-shirts and too solid to knock down.

The owner of the jewelry and watch-repair shop stands in his doorway, arms folded on his chest, and looks up and down the sidewalks that have been freshly paved with wobbly bricks.

. . . . . .

The End of the World 207

Business is terrible, but what can he do? Close up and go home and watch television? Every day he waits for watches to mend. He will lock up at six. Everyone locks up at six, and most of the gas stations are closed on Sunday.

Directly below me, in the center of the broadest cow pasture, an enormous new house has just been finished and sits in its sea of mud reflecting the westering sun. Either someone has already moved in or the developer has the lights on a timer, because at dusk it suddenly shines forth like a beacon, big enough and bright enough so that planes coming in to land at Dulles can steer by it. Soon there will be houses as far as I can see. I will stand here on the deck and look out over sixty miles of suburbs with no center of gravity or source of nourishment.

Sixty miles of people with no work to do where they live and no place to live where they work.

The towns buried among them, if we can still find them at all, will rattle in the wind like the dry shells of cicadas after the creatures have departed. In North Hill the two pretty white churches, the diner, and the general store will be surrounded on all sides by thousands of strangers who don't need them, who will scarcely even know that this was once a town.

The towns mattered only when their neighbors needed them, but each had its reason and still has its story and its own recurring family surnames painted on the outlying mailboxes. When you're there, you know where you are. How shall we ever learn to tell Heritage Farms from Mountainvue Estates? How will the executives find their way home, or even know they've found it when they get there?

Will the ghosts of peach trees push up through their carpeting? Will the executives keep hearing cows and roosters in their sleep, and wake confused and pad over to the window to reassure themselves with the sight of houses clustered all around, burglar lights ablaze?

I MOVED into this world blindly, like a cat brought in a cat carrier, and looked around and sniffed its furniture and corners like a cat in a strange room. I settled in and studied local weather and learned to be content here. Nobody said my new world itself was going to leave.

Come from away, I haven't any right to complain. There are people here selling and leaving whose families loved this place for 250 years, people who feel that leaving is a kind of death. But when a place isn't a place at all anymore, why stay?

I was told as a child to eat what was put on my plate and usually I do, feeling that possibly whatever put it there knows what's good for me better than I do. So I came, taking it for a sort of calling. It would have been more dignified if I'd been called to walk barefoot through Amazonia converting the Indians or chaining myself to the last rosewood trees. Just being called to live alone on a modest mountain in northern Virginia was harder because the challenges were so daily and so ordinary — feeding myself, keeping a grip on my friends, holding my spirits up, struggling with winter. I can't even admire myself for courage, let alone accomplishment, but at least I did what was asked.

I could try to sell. The zoning laws on the mountain are strict, but zoning in the county is so easily, almost automatically, overturned now that it scarcely seems to matter; all a developer needs to do is ask. Maybe someone would buy the land. Bulldoze the inadequate little house. Build new ones to loom commandingly over the valley.

SOMEWHERE OUT OF SIGHT in the woods below me a girl-child goes by singing. One of C. J.'s granddaughters, probably, singing to keep herself company on the long lane. The song seems to have no recognizable tune, but it's always nice to hear someone singing alone.

And after all, my house is still here, and maybe I'm meant to stay in it. Maybe I'm supposed to watch what's happening; take notes. End my days as an eccentric holdout from forgotten times, the crazy old witch on the haunted mountain with a pet pig, a shotgun across my knees, and a plug of Red Man in my cheek, reminding strangers of something they don't remember. Maybe I will.